SPIRITUAL DISCIPLINES SERIES

CONTEMPLATIVE BIBLE READING

Experiencing God Through Scripture

A SMALL GROUP DISCUSSION GUIDE

RICHARD PEACE

D0037279

NAVPRESS

BRINGING TRUTH TO LIFE

NavPress Publishing Group

P.O. Box 35001, Colorado Springs, Colorado 80935

Pilgrimage Publishing, Hamilton, Massachusetts

ISBN 08910-98992

Cover illustration: Wood River Gallery

Printed in the United States of America

1 2 3 4 5 6 7 8 9 10 / 99 98 97 96

Contents

Acknowledgments

I have always been fascinated by the Bible and how it works in us to bring about transformation. I have some clues that help me understand this process. For one thing, I know that the Bible forms our minds. Its core concepts have the ring of truth and thus help define our world view. Second, the Bible helps us in the expression of our emotions so that we can develop into more whole people than we would be otherwise. Third, the Bible shapes our behavior by giving us abundant examples of outcomes—good, bad, and indifferent—and so we learn to distinguish between behavior that brings life and behavior that brings darkness. Finally, (and perhaps most important of all) the Bible tells us that love is at the core of life. God is love. We are to love. We are loved. And so we are empowered to live life with gusto. How all this (and so much more) works together on our lives, over time, is the mystery. The testimony of countless men and women down through the ages is that it does work.

I have had the privilege of working with the Bible in a variety of ways, ranging from writing small group Bible study materials to teaching the Bible in both church and seminary. My doctoral work was done in the area of biblical studies. However, it is only rather recently that I have "discovered" contemplative Bible reading (its more common name is the Latin *lectio divina*) and this has been most illuminating. (See page 7.)

In this book, in particular, I need to acknowledge my sources, because I feel myself to be such a novice when it comes to lectio divina. Norvene Vest's book *Bible Reading for Spiritual Growth* provides the basic structure for doing group lectio. *Too Deep for Words* by Thelma Hall has been a helpful guide for me. Dom Jean Leclercq made monastic culture come wonderfully alive in *The Love of Learning,* and the *Desire for God* by Brian Taylor (Spirituality for Everyday Living) made Benedictine spirituality clear and contemporary. William Shannon's book *Seeking the Face of God* is as good a resource as I know for explaining the whole process.

I especially want to thank Father Bill Lowe of the Parish of the Messiah in Newton, Massachusetts for pointing me in the right direction in exploring lectio divina. He came to me for consultation on small groups and I received, in return, consultation on lectio divina. I also want to thank my wife Judy Boppell Peace who is involved in all my writing projects, but in this series she has gone one step further and worked through the drafts in detail. Her ability to identify just the right word has made this book more precise and clearer theologically. Finally, I want to thank Father John Kerdiejus, S. J., a spiritual friend and counselor who first introduced me to lectio divina and to so much more in the spiritual life.

The Study Guide at a Glance

What's it all about?

- This is a small group program in which you learn a spiritual discipline called contemplative Bible reading.
- Contemplative Bible reading is a way of approaching Scripture not just to learn about God but to engage in conversation with God.

How will we know what to do?

- The process of contemplative Bible reading is explained in the Introduction.
- In the first chapter, complete instructions are given for each aspect of the small group experience.

What will I learn?

- A method of Bible study that has been used by the church for over 1,500 years and that unlocks Scripture in profound ways.
- A way of prayer that flows directly from Scripture and opens up new ways of hearing God.
- A series of insights into the nature of the spiritual life drawn from the various passages of Scripture which you will study.

Is this course intended only for people who go to church?

- No—anyone can join. God is active in every life whether we acknowledge that fact or not. This group will help those not yet actively following God to see and understand God's activity in their lives, and thus to respond to God in new ways.
- This course is written in ordinary language so that anyone can participate. When theological terms are used, they are generally explained.

For how long will the small group meet together?

- This depends on the group. There is material in this book for fourteen sessions: seven Bible studies and seven small group contemplative Bible reading exercises.
- However, you can combine both parts into one session, and do the course in seven weeks.

How long does each small group session last?

- Ninety minutes per session is best. However, if necessary, you can complete the session in sixty minutes.

What if I do not know much about Bible study?

- No problem. The questions will help unlock the passage for you and the Bible study notes will give you the necessary background information.

Who leads the meetings?

- Anyone can be the leader. Beginning on page 87, there are notes about small group leadership in general as well as specific notes for each session that describe what the leader needs to do.
- However, like anything else, the more experience the better. If you have an experienced small group leader, take advantage of his or her skills.

What kind of commitment is needed?

- Each person needs to be open to the process of contemplative Bible reading, and be willing to open themselves to the text.

What happens to the group when it finishes this book?

- The group is invited to continue, using another book in the SPIRITUAL DISCIPLINES series. See "What It's All About: An Introduction to the Series" for the other titles.
- On pages 80–81 there are suggestions for continuing as a group.
- Call toll free 1-800-476-8717 for suggestions of other materials.

A Small Group Covenant

- **Attendance:** I agree to be at the meeting each week unless a genuine emergency arises.
- **Preparation:** I will do daily lectio as I am able and share with the group some of what I find.
- **Participation:** I will enter enthusiastically into the group discussion and sharing. I will participate in the group lectio experiences willingly.
- **Prayer:** I will pray for the members of my small group and for our experience together.
- **Confidentiality:** I will not share with anyone outside the group what is said during the group session.
- **Honesty:** I will be forthright and truthful in what I say.
- **Openness:** I will be candid with others in appropriate ways. I will allow others the freedom to be open in ways appropriate for them.
- **Respect:** I will not judge others, give advice, or criticize.
- **Care:** I will be open to the needs of each person in appropriate ways.

Signed: _____ **Date:** _____

Contemplative Bible Reading

The Bible stands at the center of all traditions of Christian spirituality. The question is not whether one should study the Bible (everyone agrees that we should). The question is how to study the Bible so that it shapes and forms us. Here is the challenge and here is where there are a variety of approaches. Contemplative Bible reading is one such approach that can access Scripture in a life-changing way.

Contemplative Bible reading is not a new methodology. In fact, it dates back to at least the fourth century, making it one of the oldest methods of Bible study. The traditional name for this way of reading the Bible is *lectio divina*. This is a Latin phrase (which is pronounced lex-ee-oh di-vee-nuh) which can be translated "divine reading," "spiritual reading," or "sacred reading." Lectio divina was used by monks from the earliest days of that tradition. The terms "contemplative Bible reading" and "lectio divina" (or lectio—its shortened form) will be used interchangeably in this book.

Interestingly, contemplative Bible reading is being rediscovered. As we move out of an Enlightenment era way of thinking, with its emphasis on the mind; into the Postmodern era, with its emphasis on the whole person, there is a growing desire to know the Bible in more than just a cognitive way. The fact that contemplative Bible reading has holiness of life as its objective is of great interest to people in our culture. Understanding the text is part of contemplative Bible reading, but its primary focus is on helping us to hear God's word through the text. In fact, contemplative Bible reading is really a form of prayer, as will become clear from a description of the process.

The Process of Contemplative Bible Reading

Contemplative Bible reading is both a simple and a profound way of approaching Scripture. It consists of a four-part movement, beginning with the text and ending in prayer. This way of Bible reading can be used by both individuals and groups.

The four movements that make up contemplative Bible reading are:

- **Reading/Listening:** Read aloud a short passage of Scripture. As you read it, listen for the word or phrase that speaks to you. What is the Spirit drawing your attention to?

- **Meditating:** Repeat aloud the word or phrase to which you are drawn. Make connections between it and your life. What is God saying to you by means of this word or phrase?

- **Praying:** Now take these thoughts and offer them back to God in prayer, giving thanks, asking for guidance, asking for forgiveness, and resting in God's love. What is God leading you to pray?

- **Contemplating:** Move from the activity of prayer to the stillness of contemplation. Simply rest in God's presence. Stay open to God. Listen to God. Remain in peace and silence before God. How is God revealing himself to you?[1]

Each of these four aspects of contemplative Bible reading will be discussed in more detail in the essays at the end of each chapter. However, you will learn more about each step by their practice than by their definition. This is the aim of the small group sessions: to learn, together with a group of like-minded people, how to do contemplative Bible reading. In addition, you are invited to practice this process on your own during the week between small group sessions. Texts are suggested and guidance is given in each chapter for what is called daily lectio.

The Experience of Contemplative Bible Reading

Here is an example of what takes place in this process:

- **Reading/Listening:** The text chosen is Matthew 11:28–30: "Come to me, all you who are weary and burdened, and I will give you rest. Take my yoke upon you and learn from me, for I am gentle and humble in heart, and you will find rest for your souls. For my yoke is easy and my burden is light." As you read these words aloud, you are struck by the phrase "you who are weary and burdened." Your heart responds to these words. You are, indeed, weary and burdened.

- **Meditating:** Now you speak these words aloud. You turn them over in your mind: "you who are weary and burdened." Why are you so weary? Because of all the work you have done and all the work that is yet to be completed before you can rest. As you let these thoughts take hold in your mind you realize that this is not only a description of your present moment but a description of your whole life. Life has always felt burdensome to you. You have always needed to "get things done" because by your accomplishments you gain praise from others. And this praise from others has made you feel valued. You let these thoughts go where they lead you, staying in God's presence and coming back again and again to the phrase "you who are weary and burdened."

• **Praying:** Now you start formulating your prayer to God. In fact, it formulates itself even as you meditate on this phrase. You thank God for this insight into your life; for this new understanding of why you always feel so weary, so burdened. You ask God for guidance so that you can put your work into perspective: doing what needs to be done, doing what God calls you to do, and yet knowing when to say "enough." You ask God for a new sense of his love for you that will free you from your need to gain affirmation from others. You praise God for his love for you.

• **Contemplating:** As you remember again the love of God, you rest in that love. "I love you, Lord" and with those words you sit in silence before God. It is an alert silence, however. You have no agenda. You have no further words. You have already prayed. You simply sit before God. What happens in this moment of contemplation is completely up to God.

When your attention begins to wander, you go back to the text and start the process over again, listening for a new word or phrase. You read it again, listening for what else God might have for you. Or you end your prayer experience with a "thank you" or "praise God" and enter into the tasks of the day, taking with you this sense of God's presence, this experience of God's love and guidance. This "presence" sits in the background as you greet others or start work on the report you must finish that day. It sustains you in your tasks. It softens you with others. It takes the edge off the urgency that so often makes you feel burdened. You live in the world of sense and time, but with the impression of eternity in your heart.

Group Lectio Divina

It is possible to use the contemplative Bible reading process in groups as well as individually. The name for this is group lectio divina (or group lectio). This is a four-step exercise led by a small group leader which consists of multiple readings of a short text, individual reflection on that text, brief sharing of this reflection with the small group, and prayer for one another.

The methodology of group lectio that you will use is based on the book *Bible Reading for Spiritual Growth* by Norvene Vest (Harper San Francisco, 1993). You are encouraged to read for yourself her full description of group lectio. Particularly illuminating is Vest's ongoing case study of a small group learning to do lectio together.

The process of group lectio is as follows:

1. Listen to the Word of God
   - As the passage is read twice, listen for the word or phrase that strikes you. During the silence each person repeats that phrase softly (or silently) to themselves.
   - Then, when invited, each person says aloud to the group this word or phrase without comment or elaboration.

2. Ask "How is my life touched by this word?"
   - The passage is read again. This is followed by personal meditation on how this word or phrase connects to your life.
   - Then, when invited, each person states in one or two sentences the connection between the phrase and their lives.

3. Ask "Is there an invitation for me to respond?"
   - After the passage is read a third time each person ponders whether they are being encouraged to do something in response.
   - This is shared briefly with the others.

4. Pray for one another to be able to respond to this invitation.
   - Each person prays briefly for the person on his or her right.

Further instructions for this process are given in chapter 1 (pages 23–24).

Group lectio differs somewhat from individual or daily lectio divina mainly because contemplation (step four) is not something one can order up or organize. Contemplation simply happens—in various ways and at various times for various people. So group lectio ends with prayer for one another and *not* in a silent resting in the presence of God.

There is another difference between daily lectio and group lectio: the invitation to action. In individual lectio, during meditation, you may or may not sense that God is calling you to respond in some deliberate way in the next day or two. But this is the essence of step three in group lectio. There is great power in asking God what he requires of us. There is great power, then, in sharing what we hear with others who join us through their prayer in helping us respond to this invitation.

Despite these differences, the essence of contemplative Bible reading is contained in group lectio: hearing a short passage, listening for a word or phrase, meditating on this word or phrase, and opening oneself up to God to respond as God leads you. The added advantage of group lectio is that what you hear can be discussed, immediately, with others who are likewise listening for God. Furthermore, by speaking aloud the invitation we feel God is giving us, we make public our intentions and the group holds us accountable in a gentle sort of way.

The premise of the SPIRITUAL DISCIPLINES series is that, given our busy lifestyles, we are more apt to learn such disciplines in a group than on our own. This also holds true for contemplative Bible reading. The experience of group lectio introduces us to the process. The practice of daily lectio deepens our understanding of the process. And the context of the small group both motivates us to practice lectio and gives us a forum in which to share what we hear from God.

Several issues are raised by group lectio. For one thing, does God always have something for us to do? Step three seems to assume so. It is important, therefore, to understand that while we may hear a call to action we may also hear a call to rest in God. Or our invitation might be to experience God's creation, or to experience the love of God.

There is a second issue that must be faced: How comfortable are you in discussing what is, fundamentally, an intimate relationship with God? It is one thing to open yourself to God; it is another to share it with others. In response to this issue, it is important to notice the way in which the sharing is structured. In group lectio, what you are asked to share is minimal. When you read the complete instructions for group lectio in chapter 1 (pages 23–24) you find that you are only asked to say aloud a few words or sentences. Furthermore, you are always given the option of "passing," that is, of saying nothing. So while public sharing lies at the heart of group lectio, it is not forced or excessive. However, as you grow in love and trust in your small group, you will find the power there is in mutual sharing. Your words will be received by the group as a gift to them; you will experience the words of others as a gift. There will be mutual growth and encouragement. This is how we are meant to live the Christian life.

Bible Study and Lectio

When we are introduced to the whole idea of lectio divina one common reaction is that this seems to take away the objective study of Scripture and replace it with a highly subjective method of interpretation. This has the potential to stray far from the original meaning of the text. It is a legitimate criticism and one that needs to be taken seriously. There has been an unfortunate history of making the Bible mean whatever a person wants it to mean. When one considers the range of behavior and ideas that Scripture is supposed to support—many which are contradictory to each other—the problem is identified. The need for careful Bible study is clear. When examining Scripture the first question must always be: What did the passage mean to those who originally read it? The sole question can never be: What does the passage mean to me?

But subjectivism is not the only problem. The objective can also get out of hand. Too much Bible study these days has been reduced to a mere academic exercise in which hypotheses are weighed and tested, various interpretations are discussed, and in the end people know a lot more about a passage, but it makes little difference to how they live.

The choice ought not to be between dry scholasticism and irresponsible subjectivism. We need both approaches to Scripture. We need analysis and we need application. We need knowledge and we need insight. We need to listen with our minds and we need to hear with our hearts. If the Bible is, as we claim, the inspired Word of God, then we need to approach it so as to understand what God is saying to us, and to hear God say this to us in the context of our lives.

This is the approach in this book. Each chapter consists of two small group sessions. The first session is serious Bible study. The attempt is made to understand what the text is saying. Bible study notes are included which give contextual data to assist in the process of accurate understanding. The second session in the chapter then builds on this insight, and (by means of group lectio) invites group members to listen with their hearts to what their heads know. Neither process is done to the exclusion of the other. In the first small group session, analysis ends with application. The question is asked: In what ways does this text resonate with my life? Likewise, at the end of the small group lectio session there is discussion in which the wisdom of the group is brought to bear on what we hear from God. A word from God must be tested out with committed others. This is the process of group discernment. What we attempt to do in this study guide is a kind of balanced Bible study that takes with utmost seriousness both the need to analyze and the need to listen; the need to understand and the need to pray.

---

[1]The Bible generally uses masculine language (and occasionally feminine terms)—not to imply gender but to indicate personhood. Some Christians are offended by strict masculine language (knowing that the God of the Bible is not male or female). Others are offended by gender neutral language. I have chosen to use traditional masculine pronouns on those occasions when they are required but I recognize that God is not male and that the English language is deficient at this point.

How It Works: A Brief Guide on How to Use Each Section of the Chapter

- **Overview:** This section gives you a preview of what you will find in the chapter.

- **Open:** Your main aim in this exercise is to begin the process of group building. A group of acquaintances become a group of friends as you tell your stories to one another.

- **Bible study:** The first small group session in each chapter is a Bible study in which you examine a passage that touches upon the spiritual life in some way. In this Bible study you will understand the text in new ways and identify the connection it makes to your daily life. A series of Bible study notes that give you background information about the passage will assist you in this process of analysis and reflection. Following each note is a section (called Connections) that defines its twentieth-century application.

- **Group lectio:** In the second small group session a portion of the text that you studied is used as the basis for a group lectio exercise. The small group leader will guide you step-by-step through this four-part process.

- **Discussion:** The purpose of this final portion of the session is to discuss both the experience of lectio and the outcomes. At first when you are learning this method, you will want to focus on the process itself. Later, you may want to use this time for more discussion of personal outcomes. The time for the discussion section is adjustable. How long the group lectio takes will depend upon how many people you have in the group. Take as much time as you need for the group lectio, and use the remaining time for discussion.

- **Essay:** The essay in each chapter examines a different aspect of contemplative Bible reading. The process itself is described in the Introduction. These essays expand your understanding of each aspect of contemplative Bible reading. They are to be read on your own though some groups may choose to discuss them together.

- **Daily lectio:** You will learn how to engage in contemplative Bible reading by practicing this discipline on your own. Suggestions will be given for texts that you can examine during the week between small group sessions.

The Process of Group Lectio

1. Prepare.
   - Sit in silence with your eyes closed, let your body relax.
   - Focus on God. You may wish to use a centering prayer such as "Lord Jesus Christ, have mercy" or "Come, Lord Jesus."

2. Listen to the Word of God.
   - As the passage is read twice, listen for the word or phrase that strikes you.
   - During the one minute of silence that follows the second reading, repeat that phrase softly (or silently) to yourself.
   - The leader says "Let us share our words or phrases" and begins by sharing his or her phrase. When it is your turn in the circle, speak your phrase aloud. Say only this word or phrase with no comments or elaboration.
   - You may say "I pass" if you wish, at any point in this process.

3. Ask "How is my life touched by this word?"
   - The passage will now be read again (by a different person).
   - Consider how this word or phrase connects to your life. Sometimes this will be an idea or a thought; at other times it will be an image or some other impression.
   - You will have two to three minutes of silence for this meditation.
   - The leader will say, "Let us share our reflections" and share his or her impression. When it is your turn, share in one or two sentences the connection between your phrase and your life. Again, do not elaborate, explain, or justify what you sensed.

4. Ask "Am I being invited to respond?"
   - The passage will now be read a third time (by yet another person).
   - Consider whether you are being invited to respond in some way in the next few days: "Am I being encouraged to do something?"
   - You will have two to three minutes of silence for meditation.
   - The leader will say, "Let us share our invitation" and will begin the sharing. When it is your turn, share in one or two sentences, without elaboration, the invitation you are being given.
   - Listen carefully to what the person on your right says since you will pray for that person based upon what he or she has shared.

5. Pray for one another to be enabled to respond to this invitation.
   - The leader will begin by praying for the person on the right.
   - When your turn comes pray briefly for the person on your right.
   - You may pray aloud or silently. If you pray silently, say "Amen" when you finish so the next person will begin praying.

The Longing for God

Overview

You will introduce yourself in the first small group session by talking about your experience of Bible study and your interest in the topic of contemplative Bible reading. The passage you will study together is Psalm 63 which speaks of our longing for God. The essay focuses on the history of this spiritual discipline. The more you know about the roots of contemplative Bible reading, the better able you are to practice it.

Small Group Session One

Open (20/30 minutes)

Studying the Bible:

Each of us brings to this small group experience our own experience of the Bible. By way of introducing yourself to the group, think about the many ways you have encountered the Bible.

1. Introduce yourself to the group:
   - Briefly describe one amazing incident in your life or exciting experience you have had (e.g., one summer you hiked through the Grand Tetons; OR you were born in South Africa; OR you raised four children; OR you touched a shark while diving).
   - Give one reason why you came to this particular small group.

2. Identify all the ways in which you have learned about the Bible. Which has been the most meaningful for you? Why?

❏ through sermons	❏ in Christian education classes
❏ through personal study	❏ through continuing education
❏ in small groups	❏ at a retreat
❏ in quiet times	❏ in a college or seminary class
❏ by reading commentaries	❏ through devotional reading
❏ in family readings	❏ as great literature
❏ other: _____	

3. If possible, share one experience in which the Bible came alive for you in a special way.

The Passage (5 minutes)

A psalm of David. When he was in the Desert of Judah.

> ^{1}O God, you are my God,
>   earnestly I seek you;
> my soul thirsts for you,
>   my body longs for you,
> in a dry and weary land
>   where there is no water.
>
> ^{2}I have seen you in the sanctuary
>   and beheld your power and your glory.
> ^{3}Because your love is better than life,
>   my lips will glorify you.
> ^{4}I will praise you as long as I live,
>   and in your name I will lift up my hands.
> ^{5}My soul will be satisfied as with the richest of foods;
>   with singing lips my mouth will praise you.
>
> ^{6}On my bed I remember you;
>   I think of you through the watches of the night.
> ^{7}Because you are my help,
>   I sing in the shadow of your wings.
> ^{8}My soul clings to you;
>   your right hand upholds me.
>
> ^{9}They who seek my life will be destroyed;
>   they will go down to the depths of the earth.
> ^{10}They will be given over to the sword
>   and become food for jackals.
>
> ^{11}But the king will rejoice in God;
>   all who swear by God's name will praise him,
>   while the mouths of liars will be silenced.

Psalm 63 (NIV)

Analysis (10/15 minutes)

1. Using a word or a phrase, identify the theme of each of the four
   sections of this Psalm:

   • Verse 1   _____

   • Verses 2–5   _____

   • Verses 6–8   _____

   • Verses 9–11   _____

2. Section One (verse 1):
   - What is the central image David uses to describe his longing for God (verse 1)?
   - Think about your worst experience of thirst. What does that teach you about the kind of longing David had for God?
   - How does David describe his relationship with God?

3. Section Two (verses 2–5):
   - What experiences does David name in which he has encountered God?
   - What are his various responses to God?
   - What is the outcome of this experience with God?

4. Section Three (verses 6–8):
   - Why would night be a time of particular terror for David?
   - What did he do during the night?
   - What attitudes toward God enabled him to get through the night? What images does he use to describe these attitudes?

5. Section Four (verses 9–11):
   - Who do you suppose sought David's life?
   - What outcome does David visualize? What will be the fate of his enemies?
   - What will be the response of the friends of God?

Resonance (20/30 minutes)

1. Longing for God:
   - In what ways have you experienced a longing for God? Explain.
     - ❏ a hunger to know God
     - ❏ a thirst for spiritual things
     - ❏ an uneasiness that is not satisfied by external things
     - ❏ an intimation of God that whets your appetite
     - ❏ an inner desire for the transcendent
     - ❏ a holy restlessness
     - ❏ a calling to be about God's work
     - ❏ an urgency to grasp what is real
     - ❏ dreams from God
     - ❏ a pain that is too deep
     - ❏ a longing to touch the life of God
     - ❏ other: _____
   - How is God revealing himself in your life these days?

2. Experiencing God:
   - In what ways have you experienced God?

     ☐ in Scripture   ☐ in community with others
     ☐ in nature   ☐ through the still, small voice
     ☐ in prayer   ☐ in contemplation
     ☐ in worship   ☐ in deeds done for others
     ☐ in a dream   ☐ in the events of life
     ☐ in my meditation   ☐ in a mystical experience
     ☐ in a charismatic experience ☐ in the inconsolable longing
     ☐ in a sense of "oughtness" ☐ in relationships
     ☐ in the fruits of the Spirit

   - What ways of responding to God have been most meaningful?

     ☐ worship   ☐ singing
     ☐ praise   ☐ in prayer
     ☐ through words   ☐ in bodily action (hands, dance)
     ☐ in fellowship with others ☐ in quiet meditation
     ☐ in creative responses   ☐ in sharing God's story
     ☐ in acting on behalf of others ☐ through spiritual disciplines
     ☐ in turning away from darkness
     ☐ in beholding the works and wonders of God
     ☐ other: _____

3. Night Terrors:
   - What are nights like for you?
   - What problem does night present to you? How do you cope?
   - In what ways might David's words help you at night?

4. Life Destroyers:
   - What are the names of those forces or powers that take life from you? (Examples include such things as lust, addiction, lies, despair, hatred).
   - How does David's vision of the End help us in resisting these life-taking forces?

Prayer (5/10 minutes)

1. Go around the group and ask each person to identify in thirty seconds or less one thing God has been saying to him or her personally out of this study.

2. Go around the circle a second time and let each person pray for the small group member on his or her right, based on what that person just shared about the impact of the text.

Bible Study Notes

Overview:

Context: David was in big trouble when he wrote this Psalm. His son Absalom had mounted a coup to take over the throne. David had fled into the desert (2 Samuel 15). In the midst of his distress, the faith of David is apparent as is his longing for God. Psalm 63 begins with longing (verse 1) but ends with rejoicing (verse 11).

Connection: Various themes are struck in this Psalm that are much like our own issues: longing for God, our experience of God, terrors that confront us, forces that have the potential to undo us, hope that sustains us in the midst of trial. Identify which of these connect most deeply with your life.

Verse 1:

Context: David's longing for God is so intense that he compares it to the kind of physical deprivation one feels in a hot, desolate desert without water. "A dry and weary land" is an apt description of the wild, hostile range of hills and deserts in the region between Jerusalem and the Jordan. "You are my God" is a strong and certain assertion of the deepest reality for David.

Connection: The physical language used to describe this longing may not be just a metaphor but actual. This is what it really feels like to desire God in the depth of one's being: it is a deep thirst.

Verse 2:

Context: David's flight into the desert has denied him access to the temple and to the worship of God which took place there. But he remembers what it was like. The very power and glory of God was a palpable presence in the innermost part of the Temple. This "power" is the influence or force that God exerts. His "glory" is his presence. Its substantial nature makes God so much more real than anything or anyone else. His "weight" or "thickness" gives him substance against which everything else is fleeting and inconsequential.

Connection: Have you experienced worship to this degree? Who is God to you in worship?

Verses 3–4:

Context: What David remembers most of all is the special quality of God's "steadfast love" or "lovingkindness" (phrases which translate the Hebrew word *chesedh,* used here). This Hebrew word is used frequently in the Old Testament and is difficult to translate fully into English. It speaks of an enduring love on God's part, love that will not let you down, love that flows out of God's faithfulness in keeping his promises to us. This is a love so powerful that to know it is better than life itself.

Connection: To experience the love of God is the longing of the spiritual person. This is our goal in contemplation: to rest in the presence of that love. When we know we are loved by God, we are empowered by the joy which expresses itself in deep praise.

Verse 5:

Context: So satisfying is his experience of God in worship that David uses another physical image to express what it means to him. His soul is as satisfied with the power, glory, and steadfast love of God as his body is satisfied when he eats the richest of foods. David's praise to God is expressed with his lips (through words), by his raised hands, and in his singing.

Connection: How do you worship God?

Verses 6–8:

Context: Night in the desert is a dangerous time. Not only is David at risk from nocturnal creatures, but this is also the time when his enemies can sneak up on him. So he does not sleep well. He must keep watch. But he is sustained during these lonely, dark hours by his meditation: his remembrance of God. Two images express his confidence. God is to him like a bird sheltering its chick under its large, comforting wings. God holds him in his mighty hand where no harm can befall him.

Connection: It is not uncommon for "night thoughts" to afflict us as we try to sleep: the anxieties we keep in check during the day emerge as troubling thoughts when we let down our guard. We remember tasks we have to complete, encounters that grieve us, fears that overwhelm us. David gives us a way to cope with night thoughts. We center our thoughts on God and not on these troubles. We give our anxiety over to God. We remember God.

Verses 9–11:

Context: His thoughts are on those enemies who stalk him by night. David envisions a future when all this is over, he is vindicated by God, and his enemies have met destruction. Though he thinks of the positive outcome, his words anticipate the Christian hope that one day this world with all its woes will end when Jesus returns a second time and the world is transformed into a new heaven and a new earth where righteousness prevails. David here envisions a great battle at the conclusion of which his dead enemies lie unburied on the battle field, where they are food for scavengers. In verse 11 he speaks of his victory and the rejoicing this will bring from him and from those who also follow God.

Connection: For the Christian, the future—God's future—is a great comfort. Though times may be hard now, we know that ultimately we have a home with God and this makes it possible to go on. This is not "pie in the sky by and by" but a strong faith in God.

We, too, may have enemies who seek to take life from us, figuratively if not literally. Examples of "enemies" which take life from us are: a demanding parent who is unwilling that we should live our own lives; a culture that demands we hate those who are not like us or who are not from our tribe or group; a job that demeans us daily by the lies it requires from us for success.

Small Group Session Two

Open (20/30 minutes)

Listening to God

Almost everyone prays. How, when, and why we pray varies greatly. What have your prayer experiences been like?

1. When you were a child, how did you pray? Are your memories of such prayer positive, negative, or neutral?
   - ☐ at meals
   - ☐ at church
   - ☐ with friends
   - ☐ I didn't pray
   - ☐ before going to sleep
   - ☐ in Sunday school
   - ☐ on my own
   - ☐ I heard others pray

2. What is the most remarkable answer to prayer you have heard about or experienced?

3. What role does prayer play in your life now, if any?

Group Lectio (30/40 minutes)

Your small group leader will guide you in the group lectio exercise.

The Passage

O God, you are my God,
    earnestly I seek you;
my soul thirsts for you,
    my body longs for you,
in a dry and weary land
    where there is no water.   Psalm 63:1

Discussion (10/20 minutes)

1. Process: This may well have been your first experience of group lectio. Think about the process itself:
   - Was this a comfortable experience for you? Why, or why not?
   - Listening: Was your word or phrase obvious? Not so obvious?
   - Meditating: Was finding connections easy or hard?
   - Hearing: Was the invitation to action easy or hard to discern?
   - Prayer: What was it like for you to pray? To be prayed for?
   - What part of the process is unclear to you?

2. Experience:
   - What happened for you in this exercise?

Essay

The History of Lectio Divina

Lectio divina is a time-tested and proven means by which to hear God and know God's will. It has been used by the church for over 1,500 years. This method of Bible reading is gaining new popularity as more and more people are finding it a powerful way to nurture their spiritual lives. In the past, (especially in the Protestant church) we have concentrated on the study of the Bible. As a result we have come to know a lot about the Bible. But we have not been very good at applying the Bible, much less hearing God through the Bible. Lectio divina is an approach that builds on serious Bible study, but moves to new depths as we open ourselves to God through the Bible.

The early monks approached the Bible by means of lectio divina. The process worked for them like this: During the time set aside for personal reading, prayer, and reflection a monk would go off to a private place and begin to repeat aloud a passage from Scripture. Often this was taken from the Psalms, or perhaps it was a gospel story. The monk spoke the passage out loud until he was struck by a particular word or phrase. Then he would stop and ponder this word or phrase, understanding it to be a word from God for him. This meditation (which is what he was doing) led naturally into prayer as the monk offered back to God what he heard. As he moved deeper and deeper into prayer he would come to the place where he rested in the presence of God. Such a state of contemplation was actively sought by monks.

One of the first leaders to commend lectio divina as a spiritual exercise was St. Benedict, an Italian monk who lived in the fifth and sixth century (ca. 480–550). He wrote *Rule for Monks* in A.D. 525 in which he outlined what life in a monastery should be like. His *Rule* quickly became the standard text that guided the functioning of monasteries.

Benedict is sometimes credited with inventing the workday. In the *Rule* he gives a detailed schedule (called an *horarium*) for a monastic day. In this schedule, lectio divina is so important that several hours each day are given over to it and it is to be undertaken at the time of day when the monks had the most mental energy. When Benedict spoke of lectio what he had in mind was that step in the process that involved "chewing" on the text. A monk would speak aloud the text and ruminate on the words he was hearing. In the twelfth century, Guigo II, a French Carthusian monk spoke of lectio as a process and not just a step. It was he who made it into the four step exercise that is made use of in this book.

Daily Lectio

As with other spiritual disciplines, you will only learn lectio divina through practice. So, if possible, take some time during the week to read and pray in this way. You will need to find between fifteen and thirty minutes in a quiet space. Then follow the outline described in the Introduction (and summarized below):

- *Prepare:* Relax physically and focus spiritually. Center your thoughts on God. Pray for guidance.
- *Read/Listen:* Read the passage aloud to yourself. Read slowly and with openness.
- *Meditate:* When a word or phrase strikes you, stop and repeat over again to yourself. Don't try to figure out why it has your attention. Be open to connections between the phrase and your life. Mull these over.
- *Pray:* Offer these thoughts to God. Respond to God. Don't worry about whether your prayer is profound or long. It may only be a word or two.
- *Contemplate:* Sit in silence before God. Listen. Be open to images or impressions.
- *Repeat:* Go back to the text when your mind starts to wander. Start reading again. Repeat the whole process.
- *Conclude:* Offer a word of thanks or praise to God.

Introduction to the Passage

The first story for you to investigate is found in Exodus 3:1–12, when Moses meets God at the burning bush.

Moses was in a difficult place when this incident occurred. He was living in a remote area, working as a shepherd, looking after the flock of his father-in-law, Jethro. This was a far cry from his former life in Egypt. There he had been a prince, now he is a hired-hand.

At the time of this incident, Moses had been shepherding his father-in-law's sheep and goats for almost forty years. On this particular day he was going about his normal routine, when he had a sudden, dramatic, and totally unexpected encounter with God himself.

We too know failure and fall, mediocrity and boredom, exile and pain, life in the wilderness. We too know that it is more often at the bottom than at the top that God comes alive for us, when everything changes, and we are given new hope, new vision, and a new task.

Work through this passage using the lectio divina method of study and prayer.

The Call of Jesus

Overview

In the first small group session you will discuss the Group Covenant which will serve as the guide to how you relate to one another as a group. In the second small group session you will be introduced to a "Check-In" exercise that asks you to share insights from your own experience with daily lectio. The essay focuses on the process of centering as you prepare to engage in contemplative Bible reading.

Small Group Session Three

Open (20/30 minutes)

Group Covenant

Every group needs ground rules by which it functions. This is particularly important in a group such as this in which you share with one another out of the intimacy of your relationship with God. Today you will begin by discussing a Group Covenant. A covenant is simply a way of agreeing to abide by a set of principles that foster openness, honesty and love.

Read the suggested covenant (page 6) and then discuss it.

- Are there any ground rules which you think should be deleted?
- Any items to be amended or added?
- When you are all agreed, sign your covenant, pray together and offer this covenant to God.

Introduction to the Passage (5 minutes)

One of the first tasks in the ministry of Jesus was to appoint twelve individuals who would join him in his ministry. Jesus had many disciples but to these twelve he gave the name apostles (Mark 3:14). In this passage we read about the first encounter between Jesus and three of the Twelve: Andrew, Simon, and (probably) Philip. The invitation to follow him that Jesus gave to them is the same invitation he offers to us today. It is an invitation that we hear not just once but many times. In fact, Jesus urges us to follow him throughout our lives. Each time we hear that call anew we recommit ourselves to him.

²⁹The next day John saw Jesus coming toward him and said, "Look, the Lamb of God, who takes away the sin of the world! ³⁰This is the one I meant when I said, 'A man who comes after me has surpassed me because he was before me.' ³¹I myself did not know him, but the reason I came baptizing with water was that he might be revealed to Israel."

³²Then John gave this testimony: "I saw the Spirit come down from heaven as a dove and remain on him. ³³I would not have known him, except that the one who sent me to baptize with water told me, 'The man on whom you see the Spirit come down and remain is he who will baptize with the Holy Spirit.' ³⁴I have seen and I testify that this is the Son of God."

³⁵The next day John was there again with two of his disciples. ³⁶When he saw Jesus passing by, he said, "Look, the Lamb of God!"

³⁷When the two disciples heard him say this, they followed Jesus. ³⁸Turning around, Jesus saw them following and asked, "What do you want?"

They said, "Rabbi" (which means Teacher), "where are you staying?"

³⁹"Come," he replied, "and you will see."

So they went and saw where he was staying, and spent that day with him. It was about the tenth hour.

⁴⁰Andrew, Simon Peter's brother, was one of the two who heard what John had said and who had followed Jesus. ⁴¹The first thing Andrew did was to find his brother Simon and tell him, "We have found the Messiah" (that is, the Christ). ⁴²And he brought him to Jesus. Jesus looked at him and said, "You are Simon son of John. You will be called Cephas" (which, when translated, is Peter).

John 1:29–42 (NIV)

Analysis (10/15 minutes)

1. John the Baptist announces Jesus (John 1:29–34)
   - What do you remember about John the Baptist? Who is he? What did he say and do?
   - What two titles does John give to Jesus (one at the beginning of his testimony, the other at the end)? What do these titles mean?
   - What do you know about Jesus from the testimony of John?

2. Two disciples follow Jesus (John 1:35–39)
   - What attracted these two to Jesus?
   - What did they do and how did Jesus respond?
   - What was the significance of their actions?

3. Andrew brings Simon to Jesus (John 1:40–42)
   - What did Andrew tell Simon and why?
   - How did Jesus respond to Simon?

Resonance (20/30 minutes)

1. Who is Jesus to you?
   - What title best sums up who Jesus is to you? Explain.

❏ Lord	❏ Son of God
❏ Master	❏ Son of Man
❏ Savior	❏ Son of David
❏ Teacher	❏ Messiah
❏ Prophet	❏ Lamb of God
❏ Other: _____	

   - What do the twin titles Lamb of God and Son of God mean to you personally?

2. Following Jesus
   - When, if ever, did you consciously start following Jesus?
   - Why did you follow Jesus? Why do you still follow Jesus?
   - In what new ways is Jesus calling you to follow him?

3. Bringing others to Jesus
   - Whom have you brought or might you bring to Jesus?
   - What have you discovered about yourself as a result of coming to Jesus?

Prayer (5/10 minutes)

1. Go around the group and ask each person to identify in thirty seconds or less one thing God has been saying to him or her personally out of this study.

2. Go around the circle a second time and let each person pray for the small group member on his or her right, based on what that person just shared about the impact of the text.

Bible Study Notes

Overview:

Context: The two central figures in this account are John the Baptist and Jesus. What we witness is the passing of the torch from John to Jesus. John the Baptist has created quite a stir in Israel. He is the first prophet in Israel in over 300 years. As a result, the country is all astir with excitement and anticipation. The crowds flock to John, many of them making a long and arduous journey to the wilderness around the Jordan River where he is baptizing. Once there they listen eagerly to his message. It is not a comfortable message. John calls them to repentance. He baptizes them in the Jordan for the forgiveness of sins. This was unheard of for Jews to be baptized in this way. The Jews understood themselves to be God's chosen people. The rite of baptism was something Gentiles underwent when they sought to become Jews. But so great was the sense of need (Israel had been a captive nation for generations) that they submitted to baptism in great numbers.

Then along comes Jesus. He too is baptized even though John hesitates (but Jesus insists). In his baptism, Jesus identifies with the sins of the people, sins for which he will soon die. With the launching of Jesus' ministry at his baptism, John's role begins to diminish. He is the forerunner. Now the one he came to announce is here. His disciples now start to become Jesus' disciples.

Connection: Whom do you follow? John the Baptist was a worthy master. His ministry pointed to God. But there are many other gurus that lead us away from God, away from spiritual health. They point toward the darkness. Sometimes we follow individuals both living and dead. Are they worthy of our allegiance? Sometimes we follow principles or axioms like "Making a buck" or "Every man for himself" or "If no one gets hurt, it is okay." Are these ideas true enough to guide our lives? Sometimes we follow dark powers, often unconsciously, such as addiction, anger, and pride—or even, powers of evil (though we might not call them that). Are these gods worthy of your allegiance? We too much choose whom we will follow.

Verses 29–31:

Context: Here John reveals why he baptizes: to announce the coming of Jesus. Here John signals that his task is coming to an end now that Jesus has come. Here John identifies who Jesus is: he is the Lamb of God. In Israel's sacrificial system, lambs were offered at the altar as substitutes for those bringing them. In a symbolic way the people's sins were washed away by the blood of these lambs who died in their place. This is an appropriate image of what Jesus would do, except he would die in the place of not just one person but in the place of all persons for all times. He would be the final, the ultimate, and the complete sacrifice.

Connection: Jesus is someone who gives himself for others. This is the ultimate demonstration of love. If we follow Christ, by implication, we too are to relate to others not as people to be used, but rather as people we love. What does it mean to you to follow the Lamb of God?

Verses 32–34:

Context: Now Jesus is revealed to be not only the Lamb of God, but also the Son of God. This is a powerful assertion: that God's own Son would be the one to die for the sins of the world. It was in the baptism of Jesus that he is revealed for who he actually is. John gives details of Jesus' baptism. It was not just baptism with water but baptism with the Holy Spirit.

Connection: Jesus is our link to God. He is not just a martyr who gives himself for others, worthy though this is. He is God's own Son. To know Jesus is to know God. In these verses we encounter the Trinity: God the Father, God the Son, and God the Holy Spirit.

Verses 35–39:

Context: Two of John the Baptist's disciples take an interest in Jesus at the urging of John. One of these two disciples is named Andrew (verse 40), the other is anonymous. Some feel the second disciple might be John, the author of this gospel who appears anonymously at other points in the gospel as "the beloved disciple." But it is more likely that the unnamed disciple is Philip (see 1:43) who was with Andrew on two other occasions in this gospel (6:5–9; 12:21–22). The response of the two disciples is to follow Jesus. In the Gospel of John, "following" connotes discipleship. Jesus confirms their discipleship by inviting them to "Come." They then spend time with Jesus as befits new disciples. He has become their teacher (or rabbi).

Connection: People become interested in Jesus in many ways. Here it is the testimony of a respected leader, John the Baptist, that launches two men into discipleship. In the next section it is the testimony of a brother who brings Simon to Jesus. How did you get interested in Jesus? How can you help others to find Jesus?

Verses 40–42:

Context: Andrew announces to his brother Simon the exciting news: they have found the Messiah. What is so stunning about this news is that Israel has been waiting for the Messiah for hundreds of years. And now Andrew declares that the waiting is over. Jesus is the Messiah. The Messiah was understood to be God's anointed one who would come to establish God's kingdom.

When Jesus meets Simon he changes his name to Peter. Jesus sees Peter's true character. In Matthew's account we learn that "Peter" means "rock" and that Jesus will build his kingdom on this rock (Matthew 16:17–19). Peter became the leader of the Twelve and the central figure in the church in Jerusalem.

Connection: What is it that we are so excited about that we cannot wait to share with those whom we love? What is our true name? When we come to Jesus, what do we discover about who we really are?

Small Group Session Four

Open (20/30 minutes)

Checking In

Rather than beginning this session with a sharing exercise as you have up to this point, you will start by taking no more than two minutes each to share what you have learned and heard as you have worked on the daily lectio experience. Sharing can focus on:

- What are you learning about or struggling with in the lectio process?
- What are you hearing from God as you work on the passage?

Group Lectio (30/40 minutes)

Follow the group lectio process that is outlined on page 14. It is important that you stay with this process and resist the temptation to skip or add any sections. This is a time-tested process which works well when all the parts function together. Even when a section feels awkward, stay with it.

The Passage

The next day John was there again with two of his disciples. When he saw Jesus passing by, he said, "Look, the Lamb of God!"

When the two disciples heard him say this, they followed Jesus. Turning around, Jesus saw them following and asked, "What do you want?" They said, "Rabbi" (which means Teacher), "where are you staying?"

"Come," he replied, "and you will see." So they went and saw.

John 1:35–39

The Process

Follow the process that is outlined on page 14:

- Preparation/Centering
- Listen to the Word of God
- Ask "How is my life touched by this word?"
- Ask "Am I being invited to respond?"
- Pray for one another to be enabled to respond to this invitation.

Discussion (10/20 minutes)

Use this discussion time to begin the process of group discernment. That is, talk together about what you are hearing from God. This is important. Whenever you enter into the subjective you need the balancing effect of a group of friends and fellow pilgrims who will help you affirm what you are hearing or cause you to think carefully lest you misunderstand. We need others in the Christian life. To be a pilgrim following Jesus is not a solitary endeavor. We follow Jesus as part of a large band of other pilgrims: helping, encouraging, questioning, listening to, the others.

1. Process: Spend some time discussing the step-by-step process you followed.
   * Is any step still unclear?
   * Which step is easiest for you?

2. Experience: Spend most of the time discussing the outcomes of this exercise.
   * What are you hearing God say to you?
   * How is this connecting with your life?

Essay

Centering: Preparation for Lectio

Before you begin a lectio exercise it is usually necessary to take a few moments to focus your attention on God. Your aim is to let go of the issues and agendas that occupy your thoughts and move your mind instead to God. This is not always easy to do. Most of us live in an action-filled universe surrounded by distractions galore. So when we come into our group we bring with us all this internal baggage. The act of centering is a way to let go of our old agendas and give ourselves to a new agenda: openness to God.

There are two aspects of centering: the physical and the spiritual. How we position our bodies is important, so that there is no physical impediment to prayer. How we position our minds is important, so that we are focused on God and not on some other diverting issues.

The physical:

- *Seating:* It does not matter if you sit or kneel or stand. The important thing is for your spine to be straight but not tense. "This posture is important, for it brings the body to attention. If we slump, the mind and spirit slump as well, and then we are not attentive to the Word."[1] If you are sitting, let your weight rest on the seat of a straight-backed chair with both your feet flat on the ground. Let the chair take your weight. The aim is to remain alert, attentive, and aware.
- *Muscles:* Relax tense muscles. You can be very deliberate about this. Let the muscles in your legs relax. Feel your stomach muscles relax. Then relax your arms and chest. It is most important to relax the muscles in your throat. Tension collects there, unknowingly, for a lot of people. Relax your face muscles. To know what muscle relaxation feels like, try tensing a muscle group and then releasing it. Then try letting it relax even beyond its natural resting point.
- *Breathing:* Slow down your breathing. It is at this point that many people use a centering prayer (see the next page), praying the first phrase as you breathe in, praying the second phrase as you breathe out.

The spiritual:

- *Pray:* Ask the Holy Spirit to guide your exercise, to lead you to those words you need to hear, to make connections between the Word of God and your life, and to open you to God. Pray also that as you open yourself to the spiritual world that you will be protected from evil and surrounded by God's power and presence.
- *Focus on God:* You can do this by means of an image such as meeting Jesus on the road and talking with him; sitting beside a pool or near a mountain and breathing in the presence of God, etc. Or you might simply open yourself to God without image; simply praying in faith with expectation. Offer to God your concerns so that your focus is on God and not on your fears and problems. Ask God to take these burdens. You will sometimes find that certain issues will reappear during the lectio exercise as the text speaks in response to them.
- *Use a centering prayer:* These are brief phrases that help us focus on God. Examples include "Lord Jesus Christ, have mercy" (the so-called Jesus prayer); "Come, Lord Jesus, come"; "Hosanna in the highest"; and "O God, you are my God." Find the words that seem best for you to pray. You might want to pray this prayer in rhythm with your breathing, e.g., as you inhale pray "Lord Jesus Christ" and as you exhale pray "Have mercy."

When you engage in daily lectio on your own it may be helpful for you to find the right place. There is something about "sacred space." These are environments in which we find the quiet, the peace, and the focus that enables us to reach out to God through lectio. This sort of space differs for different people. It may be a garden, a loft, a particular chair, a chapel to which we go when we pray. Environment helps us focus.

You also want to find a place that will be free of interruptions. This is true whether you are doing group lectio or daily lectio. Consider the ways you might be interrupted and then think about how to deal with them before they happen. Get a babysitter to look after the kids during the group time, make sure the phone answering machine is on, schedule your time when you know everyone is away, etc.

It is important to remember the aim of all this preparation, namely, the full attention to God, focus on God, and expectation that you are coming into the real presence of the living God.

Daily Lectio

You may have found in your practice of daily lectio that your prayer and reflection do not always follow exactly the pattern for this exercise. You start off okay by reading the passage aloud. You do this several times until a word strikes you which you reflect on for a moment. But as you do so you remember other aspects of the passage that, in fact, interpret or amplify the word, and so you are drawn back into the text. Before you know it you are praying about several parts of the passage, not just one. Do not worry! The method is not an end in itself; it is a means to an end. Never forget that end: to know God and do his will. So as long as you remain faithful to the overall process—text-based prayer that opens your life to God—you are accomplishing what you seek. Use the four-fold process as the basic pattern from which you start, and to which you return, in order to stay focused. Use it but do not be confined by it.

In the week ahead, work through this text from John 15:9–17.

Introduction to the Passage

It is the last week of Jesus' life. He has come to Jerusalem despite warnings that he will be in great danger if he does so. It is Passover night. He has eaten the final supper he will share with the Twelve. He uses this time as a last opportunity to teach them. This is his final chance to communicate what they must know before he dies. In this poignant passage he reminds them that at the heart of his message is love. They are to love others as he loves them. He really loves them. They are not to think of themselves as servants but as his friends: special friends particularly chosen to bear rich fruit in his name.

As you read, consider carefully:
- The love of the Father
- The love of Jesus
- Loving others
- Being loved
- Being the friend of Jesus
- Being chosen
- The connection between obedience and love
- The connection between joy and love
- Bearing fruit

Work through this passage using the lectio divina method of study and prayer.

---

[1] *Spirituality for Everyday Life* by Brian C. Taylor (Collegeville, MN: The Liturgical Press, 1989), page 64.

The Cost of Discipleship

Overview

In the first small group session you will discuss "how to spend a million dollars" as a fun way of thinking about the role of wealth in our lives. The passage you will study is Mark 10:17–27, the encounter between Jesus and the rich, young ruler. In the group lectio the passage you will use is Mark 10:23,27 in which Jesus invites us to trust the God of the impossible. The essay focuses on the first step in contemplative Bible reading: the process of reading and listening to the text.

Small Group Session Five

Open (20/30 minutes)

A Million Dollars

If you had a million dollars, which you had to spend, how would you spend it? Remember the old TV series in which spending a million dollars was the challenge? Well, in this opening exercise, you get to spend a million—at least hypothetically!

1. If you had a million dollars, which you had to spend on one or more causes or projects, how would you spend it? Explain how you came to your decision.

   I would give a million dollars to:
   ❏ cancer research   ❏ buy livestock for Filipino farmers
   ❏ a housing project in Rwanda   ❏ fund a native art museum in Bali
   ❏ start a retreat center   ❏ start churches in East Java
   ❏ scholarship program for Bosnians ❏ other: _____

2. Now that you have given away a million dollars to worthy causes, you get to spend another million dollars on yourself!

   I would use a million dollars to:
   ❏ travel   ❏ buy a farm
   ❏ buy a great house   ❏ start an auto collection
   ❏ start an art collection ❏ retire
   ❏ start a retirement fund ❏ develop a wildlife sanctuary
   ❏ start my own business   ❏ other: _____
   ❏ fund my research

Introduction to the Passage (5 minutes)

It was not just the Twelve who followed Jesus. There were many others who were his disciples. At one point in his ministry the crowds who followed Jesus were so large that he had to stay outside the towns in isolated areas (see Mark 1:45; 3:7–12). We are told the story of some of these followers: Nicodemus, the member of the Jewish ruling council who came by night; Zacchaeus, who repaid those he cheated fourfold; Mary and Martha, who were good friends (and whose story we will study in chapter 4); and the so-called Rich Young Ruler, whose story we examine here. In examining how others came to Jesus we learn how we, too, come to Jesus. In the case of this young man we are confronted with the profound power that possessions have over us, and the challenge this is to the spiritual life.

> As Jesus started on his way, a man ran up to him and fell on his knees before him. "Good teacher," he asked, "what must I do to inherit eternal life?"
>
> "Why do you call me good?" Jesus answered. "No one is good —except God alone. You know the commandments: 'Do not murder, do not commit adultery, do not steal, do not give false testimony, do not defraud, honor your father and mother.' "
>
> "Teacher," he declared, "all these I have kept since I was a boy."
>
> Jesus looked at him and loved him. "One thing you lack," he said. "Go, sell everything you have and give to the poor, and you will have treasure in heaven. Then come, follow me."
>
> At this the man's face fell. He went away sad, because he had great wealth.
>
> Jesus looked around and said to his disciples, "How hard it is for the rich to enter the kingdom of God!"
>
> The disciples were amazed at his words. But Jesus said again, "Children, how hard it is to enter the kingdom of God! It is easier for a camel to go through the eye of a needle than for a rich man to enter the kingdom of God."
>
> The disciples were even more amazed, and said to each other, "Who then can be saved?"
>
> Jesus looked at them and said, "With man this is impossible, but not with God; all things are possible with God."
>
> Mark 10:17–27

Analysis (10/15 minutes)

1. The Young Man
   - Describe the young man. Who is he? What issues concern him? What type of person is he?
   - What is the value in keeping the commandments? What is the problem in keeping the commandments?
   - What is the problem of wealth? What is the value of wealth?

2. The Disciples
   - What amazes the disciples?
   - What is Jesus' response to their amazement? What does he mean by these words?

3. Jesus
   - What does Jesus feel about this young man? About the Twelve? About all who would follow him?
   - What do you learn about Jesus from this passage?
   - What do you learn about following Jesus from this passage?

Resonance (20/30 minutes)

1. What we love
   - In what ways is your story like the story of the young man?
   - What is it that sparked your interest in the spiritual life (eternal life)?

2. How we struggle
   - With which of the six issues (commandments) do you struggle, if any?
   - In what ways do you wrestle with the question of wealth: its acquisition, its maintenance, and its use?
   - In what ways are your possessions an impediment to your spiritual life? An aid to your spiritual life?

3. What Jesus says to us
   - What statement of Jesus do you identify with the most? Explain.
   - ❏ Why do you call me good? ❏ You know the commandments
   - ❏ I love you ❏ Go sell
   - ❏ Give to the poor ❏ Come, follow me
   - ❏ How hard it is to enter the kingdom of God
   - ❏ All things are possible with God

Prayer (5/10 minutes)

1. Go around the group and ask each person to identify in thirty seconds or less one thing God has been saying to him or her personally out of this study.

2. Go around the circle a second time and let each person pray for the small group member on his or her right, based on what that person just shared about the impact of the text.

Bible Study Notes

Overview:

Context: When telling this story, Luke identifies this man as a ruler (a leader in the Jewish community; Luke 18:18), Matthew tells us he is young (Matthew 19:20), and all three gospel writers say he is rich. Only Mark tells us that Jesus loved him (verse 21). The sincerity of the young man is obvious as is his feeling about Jesus (he knelt; he called Jesus "Good Teacher"). But his commitment to his possessions is even stronger.

Connection: What Jesus asks of this young man can sound harsh and unreasonable to our ears, and we struggle to make sense of his words. We are troubled by this passage because we in North America possess so much in comparison to the rest of the world. We devote so much of our energy to securing a comfortable lifestyle. And while we are often generous with our money, we are also haunted by our need for it. But the issue in this passage is not so much wealth itself, but our attitude toward it.

Verse 17:

Context: The young man calls Jesus "good," implying that some people (presumably like Jesus and like the young man himself) are moral (keep the law) and therefore deserve heaven. Jesus refuses to accept such a distinction. He has just said to his disciples (in verses 14–15) that to enter the kingdom of God we must become like little children; i.e., we must be like children in their openness and dependence. The kingdom is received by faith. In contrast, the young man wants to know "what to do." He does not yet understand that salvation is a gift to be received not a reward to be earned.

Connection: The question is not so much whether we have good feelings toward Jesus, but whether we will follow him. What is the basis on which we come to Jesus? What is the question we have for Jesus as we start (or restart) our spiritual pilgrimages?

Verses 18–20:

Context: No one can claim to be good, since only God is good. Jesus cuts to the heart of the young man's problem: equating being good with gaining eternal life. The insecurity of such a position is demonstrated in the young man's need to ask if he has eternal life even though he has really tried to be good.

Jesus refers to six of the ten commandments. These are the commandments that deal with our relationships with other people. The young ruler was apparently sincere in asserting that he had kept all these. (Jesus does not dispute his claim to have done so.) What he missed is Jesus' insistence (in the Sermon on the Mount, for example) that law-keeping involves inner attitudes as well as outer actions. It is at this level, at least, where we all fail.

Connection: Even when we know that salvation is "by grace through faith" we act as if it depended upon our efforts. But on the other hand, to say "I trust Jesus for my salvation" and then live without regard to any of his teachings is a contradiction in terms and makes our profession of faith suspect. The call is to trust Christ and to love him by obeying his commandments.

Verses 21–22:

Context: In the Old Testament riches were not considered a hindrance to spiritual pursuit. In fact, wealth was thought to be a sign of God's blessing (e.g., Job 1:10, 42:10; Psalm 128:1–2; Isaiah 3:10). But here Jesus points out that wealth can hinder participation in God's kingdom. Possessions were this man's problem, so Jesus tells him to get rid of them. Jesus contrasts treasure on earth (which he has) with treasure in heaven (which he wants). The young man professes an interest in the one (eternal life) but, when pressed, will not give up the other ("sell everything"). Jesus' words do not appear to be a universal prohibition against wealth. The primary call to this young man is not to follow poverty but to follow Jesus. However, it is a strong warning about the negative power of possessions.

The rich young ruler turns away. The demand is too great. He refuses the call to follow Jesus. He fails to become Jesus' disciple. By walking away he demonstrates Jesus' very point: that wealth can be a snare preventing us from discipleship. There is a sadness to this story both in the young man (his face fell) and in Jesus (who loved him and who comments wistfully on the power of riches over people).

Connection: When St. Anthony (who was born in A.D. 251) heard these words: "Go, sell everything . . . follow me," he understood them to be a personal call from God. So he withdrew into the desert for a life of solitude. When he emerged twenty years later, the crowds flocked to him because they recognized in him the holiness of life. St. Anthony is considered to be the father of the monastic movement.

The statement Jesus makes to the young man, "One thing you lack . . ." unlocks the truth of his life. It pinpoints the issue that impedes his following of Jesus. To follow Jesus we must turn around from what we now follow (repentance), and walk toward Jesus instead. What is the truth of your life?

Verses 23–25:

Context: The camel was the largest animal in Israel and a needle had the smallest opening. Thus the absolute impossibility of anyone (note that the reference to "the rich" is dropped here) entering the kingdom of God through his or her own efforts.

Connection: Wealth is the issue in America today. So much time and energy is given to its accumulation. So much evil is justified by its acquisition. So much pain is caused by its pursuit. It is very hard for North Americans to get the balance right between money as a good gift from God, and the love of money as the root of all evil (as Paul says).

Verses 26–27:

Context: Jesus responds to the fear expressed by the disciples. Eternal life cannot be earned by men and women but it will be given by God. The reality is that we are all dependent upon God (no one is good, no one is deserving) and that we must all rest in the good pleasure of a good God who loves us.

Connection: The call is to rest in the love of the God of the impossible.

Small Group Session Six

Open (20/30 minutes)

Checking In

Begin by checking in with each other. Take up to two minutes to share what you have been learning and hearing as you have worked on the daily lectio experience. When it comes to experiential exercises such as lectio, it is very important to process your experience with others.

Group Lectio (30/40 minutes)

Follow the process that is outlined in chapter 1 (page 14). Be sure to spend enough time preparing for the experience. Get in touch with each other in the check-in experience (above). Then take time to get in touch with God by doing the centering exercise. It is also important to take time to discuss the experience. Use your discussion to ponder what God is saying to people in the group. Listen to one another. Help one another distinguish what is of God from what is probably not of God (our compulsions and our history sometimes get in the way of hearing God accurately). Support one another.

The Passage

The passage you will use for this exercise is a compilation of Jesus' words in Mark 10:23, 27:

Jesus . . . said to his disciples, "How hard it is for the rich to enter the kingdom of God! . . . With man this is impossible, but not with God; all things are possible with God."

Discussion (10/20 minutes)

By this time the process of contemplative Bible reading should be familiar to you. So use this time to discuss what you are hearing God say to you—both from today's exercise and from the other lectio experiences. Become "friendly ears" for each another; helping each other with the struggle to know and do God's will. Also, be alert to what does not sound "of God." This is most important when it comes to a discipline such as contemplative Bible reading, that is, to offer our "hearing" up to the scrutiny of others, and to process it with them, trusting in the wisdom of the gathered community.

Essay

Step One: Reading/Listening

Lectio divina is a form of reading. It is, however, reading that focuses more on hearing than on seeing. Nowadays we read with our eyes. In fact, children are discouraged from mouthing words as they are learning to read. Vocalization slows down the assimilation process. But this was not the case in ancient days. Back then, to read was to speak aloud. Reading was done principally with the lips not the eyes. Books were meant to be heard and not just seen.

In fact, meditation was understood to be the act of repeating aloud the sacred text. The Hebrew word *haga* (which is translated "meditation") means to learn the Torah by pronouncing the words in a low voice. The words were murmured aloud so as to be assimilated within.

To understand why this was the case, it is necessary to put ourselves back into the ancient world—before printing presses. Books were scarce (since they were all handwritten) and literacy was by no means universal (though by the sixth century most monks could read and write). Those who could read did so by speaking aloud the words. Partly this was to aid in memorization. Since you could not just pull your own personal copy of the Bible off the shelf and turn to a passage, it was necessary to memorize texts. Repeated vocalization of words, phrases, and passages allowed people to own the text in their hearts. A person gained a muscular memory and an aural memory of the words and not just a visual memory.

Over time, these verbal memories of passages could be triggered by words or phrases, and not only was the passage recalled but so was the whole encounter with that passage before the Lord.

There is another reason for reading aloud. In an oral culture, reading aloud was a way to engage in dialogue. The text was read in order to be discussed with others. In the early church, when a letter from Paul arrived, it was read aloud to the assembled community and considered together.

When lectio divina was first described, it referred to this act of reading aloud. Later on (in the twelfth century to be accurate) lectio divina was made into the four-part process that we have been focusing on. But even in that process, the first step is the vocalization of sacred scripture.

So, step one in contemplative Bible reading is to read and to hear the text. In group lectio the text is read aloud four times. In daily lectio, we keep going back over the text, reading it slowly over and over again so as to listen with full intensity. It is important to listen carefully since there is a difference between hearing and listening. We hear a lot; we listen to little. When it comes to contemplative Bible reading we need to give our full attention to the text. Short passages have been chosen to facilitate such concentration. When we read, we read slowly, savoring the text, paying attention to all the words, letting the words form images in our minds.

There are times when the text does not seem to speak to you. What you hear are words only; true words, interesting words, useful words but not words that resonate. That too is fine. Repeat the text over several times until you grow familiar with it. At some later date you may be drawn back to that text. In any case, long-time practitioners of lectio divina counsel that there is value in the very act of hearing the word of God—whether or not we consciously connect with the text.

What we are doing in all this is acting upon our theology. We call the Bible the Word of God. In lectio divina we are listening to the text as the Word of God. We are listening to God's word to us and for us and among us. In doing this we are engaging in a conversation with God.

There is one final consideration when it comes to reading and hearing the text. What text do I read? Sometimes we know what we should read. The Holy Spirit brings a passage to mind. Pay attention to such intuitions. They generally lead you to what you need to hear and reflect on. However, it is more common that we are working on a text for a particular purpose: it has been suggested by a spiritual director, it is a lectionary text, it deals with an issue with which we are wrestling, it is part of a small group we belong to (as with this series). If you are looking for texts, consult Thelma Hall's book: *Too Deep for Words.* She lists 500 lectio texts grouped around fifty subjects.

Daily Lectio

In the week ahead, work through this text from Matthew 11:25–30.

Introduction to the Passage

This passage consists of three parts: a prayer of thanksgiving, a wise utterance, and an invitation from Jesus. The passage begins with a prayer of Jesus. Throughout the Gospels we hear that Jesus has prayed or is praying, and we read some of the prayers that he prays.[1] That prayer stood at the center of the spiritual life of Jesus is the strongest possible indication that prayer should be at the heart of our spiritual life. And, of course, we should remember that lectio is a process of prayer.

Following his prayer, Jesus comments on how the spiritual life functions. We are totally dependent upon the grace of God. Salvation may be impossible for us to achieve on our own, but with God all things are possible.

This passage ends with a warm and gracious invitation to us in our weariness. Jesus call us to himself. This is not a call to passivity or inaction. We are invited to take upon ourselves a "yoke." But this is not like the yoke of the law which weighs down and binds us. This is to be a yoke of gentleness and humility. This is the yoke of discipleship. It means to be bound together with Jesus in our pilgrimage.

The central image here is of a yoke. This may refer to the kind of yoke that linked two oxen together to pull a plow, or it may be the yoke placed by the victor on his captives to parade them through town. Regardless, the image is clear: we are bound by this yoke together with Jesus. But this is not a burdensome binding. Jesus' yoke is easy (because he is pulling most of the weight?) and his burden is light (unlike the weight of law which the Pharisees placed on people). This is the yoke that enlivens, not the yoke that deadens.

Work through this passage using the lectio divina method of study and prayer. _____

[1] For more information on the prayer life of Jesus read *The Prayer Life of Jesus: Shout of Agony, Revelation of Love*, by William David Spencer and Aída Besançon Spencer (University Press of America).

The Priorities of Life

Overview

In the first small group session you get to explore your personality "type." This will be good preparation for understanding the encounter between Martha and her quite different sister Mary which you will study in Luke 10:38–42. In this passage you will consider your priorities in life as you follow Jesus. The focus of the essay is on the second step in contemplative Bible reading: the process of meditation.

Small Group Session Seven

Open (20/30 minutes)

What's Your Type?

The Myers-Briggs Type Indicator (MBTI)[1] is a widely used personality test that can help you better understand yourself and the others in the group. We cannot provide the MBTI test, much less take the time to score it and explore it. But you can make a good first guess at the four letters that identify your Type.

1. What is your Type? In each of the four categories, circle the preference that most nearly fits who you are. Don't worry if the fit is only approximate.

Are you an Introvert (I) or an Extrovert (E)?　　Circle **I** or **E**
- An Introvert gets new energy by being alone; reflects on what he/she thinks before speaking; is a good listener; likes being with a few good friends; finds socializing to be draining after a while.
- An Extrovert gets new energy from being with other people; figures out what he/she thinks by talking it out; is a great conversationalist; likes parties; works best in the company of others.

Do you gather data through Sensing (S) or Intuition (N)?　Circle **S** or **N**
- A Sensor prefers specific answers to specific questions; likes jobs with visible results; works with facts rather than theories; likes clear instructions; is a literalist; focuses on the specific.

- An Intuitive juggles several thoughts simultaneously; gets excited about future possibilities; finds details boring; likes the big picture; loves puns; sees interrelationships between things.

Do you make decisions by Thinking (T) or Feeling (F)?   Circle **T** or **F** (Warning: do not interpret "feeling" here to mean "emotion.")
- A Thinker makes decisions based on what is true; is objective; is logical; prefers to be right rather than liked; is calm in conflict; likes to argue in a discussion.
- A Feeler makes decisions that take into accounts the feelings of others; senses what others are experiencing and feeling; makes decisions on the basis of values; prefers harmony to clarity; takes things personally; accommodates others.

Do you respond in a Judging (J) or Perceiving (P) way?   Circle **J** or **P** (Warning: don't try to understand these terms in their normal senses!)
- A Judger is on time; is organized; knows what others should be doing; hates surprises; makes schedules; plans ahead.
- A Perceiver has trouble with deadlines; is spontaneous; likes to keep options open; loves the unknown; responds to the moment; is flexible.[2]

2. Go around the group and share your Type. Then
- Get one I and one E to talk about what energizes them.
- Get one S and one N to talk about the role of details in life.
- Get one T and one F to talk about how to make decisions.
- Get one J and one P to talk about organizing a small group session.

3. Compare the Types of those in your group who find contemplative Bible reading easy and exhilarating and the Types of those who find it difficult and hard work. Do you see any connections between Type and preferred spiritual style?

Introduction to the Passage (5 minutes)

Many women followed Jesus. They were his disciples and his friends. This was unusual in the first century when women were considered to be mere property with few rights of their own. They were not seen as independent individuals who would make fit disciples. However, Jesus refused to be bound by these social conventions. He treated women as equals. He welcomed them as his followers in the same way he welcomed men.

In the passage we are studying, it is clear that Mary and Martha are more than disciples; they are friends of Jesus. There is a light, comfortable feeling to this scene. One can picture Jesus relaxing in their home, not pressed by the crowds wanting something from him, but in conversation with old friends about issues that matter. In their dialogue we are confronted with our need to balance work with the rest of life, and to discern what really matters in life.

As Jesus and his disciples were on their way, he came to a village where a woman named Martha opened her home to him. She had a sister called Mary, who sat at the Lord's feet listening to what he said. But Martha was distracted by all the preparations that had to be made. She came to him and asked, "Lord, don't you care that my sister has left me to do the work by myself? Tell her to help me!"

"Martha, Martha," the Lord answered, "you are worried and upset about many things, but only one thing is needed. Mary has chosen what is better, and it will not be taken away from her."

Luke 10:38–42

Analysis (10/15 minutes)

1. Jesus and Mary
   - What do you know about Mary from this passage? What kind of person is she?
   - Who do you know like Mary and what are that person's strengths and weaknesses?
   - Why is Mary commended, and how do you feel about this given the situation?

2. Jesus and Martha
   - What do you know about Martha from this passage? What kind of person is she?
   - Who do you know like Martha and what are that person's strengths and weaknesses?
   - What impact, do you suppose, did her complaint about Mary have on the dinner party?
   - Why does Jesus respond this way to Martha, and how do you feel about his response given the situation?

3. Jesus and Life
   - What does Jesus mean when he says "only one thing is needed"?

Resonance (20/30 minutes)

1. Rate the following activities according to how important they are to you, beginning with (**1**) for the most important:

   _____ Job   _____ Leisure
   _____ Study   _____ Conversation
   _____ Tasks   _____ Childcare
   _____ Church   _____ Relationships
   _____ Eating   _____ Sleeping
   _____ Television   _____ Spiritual disciplines

2. Go back over this list and indicate how much time you actually spend per day on each activity. What discrepancies, if any, are there between what you value and how you spend your time?

3. Who are you most like (Mary or Martha) in the following areas?
   * work   ❏ Mary   ❏ Martha
   * relationships   ❏ Mary   ❏ Martha
   * responsibility   ❏ Mary   ❏ Martha
   * time management   ❏ Mary   ❏ Martha
   * spiritual discipline ❏ Mary   ❏ Martha

4. What have you determined is the "one thing needed" in your life after all this conversation and analysis?

Prayer (5/10 minutes)

1. Go around the group and ask each person to identify in thirty seconds or less one thing God has been saying to him or her personally out of this study.

2. Go around the circle a second time and let each person pray for the small group member on his or her right, based on what that person just shared about the impact of the text.

Bible Study Notes

Overview:

Context: Luke is the only one who tells us this wonderful story. It provides valuable insight into how to view priorities in life. The personalities of the two women are made clear by a few deft strokes of Luke's pen. However, you can get a fuller sense of who they are by reading John 11:1–12:10. Clearly, Martha is a strong and forceful woman with a quick mind, able to hold her own with Jesus. Mary is more in touch with her feelings and more naturally relational. She is identified by John as the woman who poured expensive perfume on the feet of Jesus (which becomes an anticipation of his burial) and then wiped it off with her hair (an act which would have shocked onlookers since women did not unbind their hair in public). Lazarus is identified in John 11 as a good friend of Jesus. John also tells us that Jesus loved all three of these siblings (John 11:5). It is clear that they were close friends.

Connection: Several issues are raised in this story: the role of work in our lives; the question of how to set priorities; the conflict between siblings; the active versus the contemplative; and the role of women as disciples of Jesus.

Verse 38:

Context: Jesus is traveling with his disciples (probably the Twelve though more may have been included). Whether his disciples come with him to Mary and Martha's house is not clear though the switch to the singular ("he came to a village" and "Martha opened her home to him") may indicate that he alone stopped there. But on the other hand, it may have been that thirteen people stopped by, in which case the frantic character of Martha's preparation is better understood.

The village is not named. However, in John 11:1 we learn that Mary, Martha, and their brother Lazarus lived in Bethany, a town two miles from Jerusalem.

Connection: Jesus stopped by. This is a place he knew; a place where he was welcome; a place which offered him hospitality; and a place where he was comfortable. In other words, this is the home of good friends.

Verse 39:

Context: With these few words (plus Martha's comments in verse 40), Luke describes Mary to us. We know her, too. At least we know people like her. Her temperament is familiar. In Myers-Briggs language, Mary is a "P." She is the type of woman who responds to the moment. She would rather engage in conversation than plan a meal. She is probably fun to be with though you would not want her to organize your finances and do your taxes. She is adaptable, flexible, relational, and spontaneous but she is not goal-oriented nor an organizer.

Jesus encourages Mary in her eagerness to learn. His response would have put him at odds with the prevailing notion of the time when Jewish teachers for the most part, did not view women as learners. In fact, Johanan of

Jerusalem gave this advice: "Talk not much with womenkind." Another rabbi said: "If any man gives his daughter knowledge of the Law, it is as though he taught her lechery."

Connection: Mary is a disciple. She wants to learn from Jesus. She is eager to hear his words. She is a model of discipleship in that she chooses the kind of active reflection that goes on between teacher and student. Lectio is a way of attending to the Word of God in a way that allows it to have an impact on us.

Verse 40:

Context: Martha is distracted by the need to make preparations. The implication is that she too wanted to learn, but the pressures of hospitality prevented that. She is also annoyed that Mary is not helping; annoyed (probably) that Jesus is encouraging (or at least, allowing) this behavior; annoyed (perhaps) that she has to feed a crowd (if the disciples are there).

Here we learn about Martha. If Mary is a "P," Martha is a "J." A "J" is a person who needs control over life and who, therefore, organizes, plans, and puts a lot of energy into making things go smoothly. "J"s don't like surprises, get irritated when other people don't do things right, have a schedule, and thrive on order. "J"s can drive you crazy but they get things done.

Connection: What role does work play in your life? While the evidence is too slim to label Martha a workaholic, it is clear that in her preoccupation with preparing a meal for her guest, she is willing and able to work hard. Of course, the issue is not just work (somebody had to fix the meal), but choices (could she have prepared a simpler meal or waited to fix dinner until a lull in the conversation?). How do we choose to use our time? Are our choices always the best? Does it really need to get done? Does activity (work) play far too large a role in our lives?

A second issue has to do with the tension between siblings. Most of us know this scene firsthand. There is work to be done. One sibling gets stuck with it. The other won't help. There is anger between the two. An appeal is made to a third party to "get her to help." The familiarity of this situation is striking. What tension do you live with (or have you lived with) regarding siblings, or with your children and their relationships?

Verses 41–42:

Context: Jesus' affection for Martha comes out in his reply "Martha, Martha . . ." He invites her to calm down. Then he describes her situation for her. She is "fretting and fussing about so many things" as the New English Bible translates the phrase. The challenge for her is to step back from the pressures of the moment and think about the larger issues.

Connection: What do you fret and fuss about? Maybe the problem is that you don't fret and fuss at all so things never get done. Jesus challenges us to fit our concerns and preoccupations into larger realities. Is all our activity necessary? How has all this activity made us feel? Is it worth it? The challenge is to discern "what is better." And certainly, Mary's choice to listen to Jesus was the better way here. This story is sometimes used to promote the contemplative way over against the activist path, but this is not the issue. Clearly both modes are needed in the spiritual life. The question here is one of priorities.

Small Group Session Eight

Open (20/30 minutes)

Checking In

Take up to two minutes to share what you have been learning and hearing as you have worked on the daily lectio experience. By now the newness of the process has worn off and daily lectio has more a sense of "spiritual discipline" to it. It is when this way of reading and praying has become second nature that its work can reach deep inside of us. Sharing can focus on:

• where you are in your mastery and use of the lectio process
• the impact contemplative Bible reading is having on your spiritual life
• what you are hearing from God

Group Lectio (30/40 minutes)

Follow the process that is outlined on page 14. By now you should be comfortable with the group lectio process. This is good. Once you are familiar with the process you do not have to give much energy to "getting it right." You will be able simply to "do it." This gives you more freedom to stay open to the unknown. Remember that God is not contained by any process or technique. God is God and will act as he wants. The process is important. By it we put ourselves in a place where we can hear God. Now that you can use the process with some ease, stay open to the way in which God uses the process in your life.

The Passage

The passage you will use for this exercise is a compilation of Jesus' words in Luke 10:41–42:

"Martha, Martha," the Lord answered, "you are worried and upset about many things, but only one thing is needed. Mary has chosen what is better, and it will not be taken away from her."

Discussion (10/20 minutes)

Norvene Vest says that there are four practices that help to make Christ the center of your small group community:
• Speaking the truth in love   • Admitting strong emotions
• Listening in love   • Confidentiality

Discuss how well you are doing in each of these areas in your group. Continue your discussion of the group lectio experience.

Essay

Step Two: Meditation

Meditation is a key spiritual exercise. It lies at the heart of lectio divina. Meditation is not an esoteric art as it is sometimes thought to be. In fact, it's quite natural. It's something we engage in all the time though we may not call it by that name. Quite simply, to meditate is to think about a subject. It is to focus on a topic, turning it over in your mind until it becomes clear or until you have new insight. Meditation is a form of reflection; it is a way of learning. Meditation is rumination; it is the use of imagination to gain new insight.

What sets meditation apart (in the sense that we use it here) from everyday rumination is the subject matter. Meditation focuses on spiritual matters: the meaning of a particular verse, how to deal with a present temptation, the sense of God's presence, etc. To meditate is to make use of a natural skill for a spiritual purpose.

To meditate is to give free reign to our imaginations in order to grasp what God is saying to us in Scripture. In lectio divina, we are invited to "see" the passage, that is, to imagine what is happening: to see how people dress, to hear the conversation, to notice the color, to feel the breeze, to smell the wood smoke, to watch the motion of the crowds. We listen to Jesus speaking (rather than just read his words). In this way we are open to the experience of God's love and not just the knowledge that God loves us. Using our imagination in Bible study is a powerful way of encountering the text.

It needs to be added that some people are more adept at using their imagination in this way than others. If this form of meditation works for you, by all means use it. If not, don't worry. There are other forms of prayer appropriate for you.[3] For example, you may find it a powerful experience simply to repeat Jesus' words from the text, letting them sink into your soul. Or meditation may mean for you to write the phrase you are focusing on in your journal, then putting down related thoughts, or trying to summarize what that phrase means to you. This, too, is a form of prayer.

There is a second distinction that can be made between meditation and ordinary reflection. It is not just a question of subject matter. It is also a question of outcome. To meditate is to think about a subject in order to do it. It is to practice a thing by thinking about it. It is to desire it in your mind even as you seek to express it in your life. In other words, this is not idle rumination, but rumination with a purpose. To meditate on a text is to so understand that text that you live it out. It is to incorporate a concept into your everyday existence. This is why meditation is so valuable as a spiritual practice. It is a way of translating the Bible into life.

But it is not just connections to my life that I find in meditation. I also learn more about God. I am struck by a variety of things concerning who God is or what God is saying about himself. I feel drawn to God in a certain way. I experience the presence of God, or the love of God, or the peace of God as I meditate. So meditation is not just a means of doing, it is also a means of being.

Daily Lectio

In the week ahead work through John 4:4–26, the story of Jesus' meeting with the woman at the well.

Introduction to the Passage

Jesus meets yet another woman. To understand the impact of this conversation, it is necessary to know something about the religious, legal, and social situation of the Samaritan woman. In those days, this woman would have been marginalized due to her gender, race, and social status. As a woman, she was a second class citizen. In one prayer, men actually thanked God that they had not been born a woman! As a Samaritan, she was viewed with suspicion because Samaritans were not descended from one of the twelve tribes (even though they claimed to be). As a woman divorced many times, she was suspect. Under the law of that time there was no limit on the number of marriages (or divorces), but only men were granted a divorce. More than three marriages was seen as very bad. For her to be living with a man to whom she was not married made her a threat to other women (which probably explains why she came alone in the heat of the day for water).

Jesus will have none of this. He actually initiates the conversation with her even though most teachers would not talk to a strange woman. Jesus treats her with respect. In verse 21 he calls her "woman" which was a term of respect and affection (the same term Jesus used for his mother at the wedding at Cana). Furthermore, Jesus treats her as an equal, as an independent adult created in the image of God. He teaches her. He dialogues with her. He reveals to her who he is.[4]

But it is what Jesus offers that gives this passage significance: living water. Living water was a gift from God. It was the gift of the Holy

Spirit. Jesus not only offered living water, he claimed that it would banish thirst forever. Only the Messiah could offer that type of water. He offers this same living water to us.

Work through this passage using the lectio divina method of study and prayer.

---

[1]For more information on the Myers-Briggs Type Indicator see *Please Understand Me: Character and Temperament Types* by David Keirsey and Marilyn Bates (Del Mar, CA: Prometeus/Nemesis Book Company, 1989).

[2]This way of talking about type is based on *Type Talk* by Otto Kroeger and Janet Thuesen (Delacorte Press) as described in Oswald and Kroeger's (Alban Institute).

[3]See *Prayer and Temperament: Different Prayer Forms for Different Personality Types* by Chester Michael and Marie Norrisey (Charlottesville, VA: The Open Door, 1984).

[4]I am grateful to my wife, Judy Boppell Peace, for the research she has done on this passage and on the Mary and Martha story. The background information I have included on the two passages is drawn from her data.

The Courage of Faith

Overview

In the first small group session you get to recall great adventures you have had—as a way of imagining what it must have been like for Peter when he walked on water (Matthew 14:22–32). In this passage you are challenged to take courage, to keep your eyes on Jesus, to have faith not doubt, and thus to do what you could never have done on your own. In the group lectio the passage you will use is Matthew 14:27–29 in which Jesus invites Peter to step out and do the impossible. The focus of the essay is on the third step in contemplative Bible reading: prayer.

Small Group Session Nine

Open (20/30 minutes)

Adventures

What is the most amazing thing you have ever done? Maybe it is not walking on water (like Peter did in the story you will study) but for you it was remarkable. When we remember what we did in the past we are empowered to stride boldly into the future.

1. What is the most amazing thing you have ever done? Explain.
   ❏ An adventure (e.g., traveled to China, climbed a mountain, entered an Iron Man/Woman competition)
   ❏ A challenge (e.g., left a job, started a business, overcame an illness)
   ❏ A relationship (e.g., got married, had children, made it on your own)
   ❏ A ministry (e.g., taught junior high Sunday school, worked with AIDS patients, started a prayer group)
   ❏ A pilgrimage (e.g., became a Christian, got a spiritual director, joined an inner-city mission)

2. What made it possible for you to do this?

3. What is the challenge you are facing at this point in your life?
   I am being called to:

❏ Move	❏ Grow	❏ Believe	❏ Hang in there
❏ Hope	❏ Love	❏ Pull back	❏ Step in
❏ Start	❏ Stop	❏ Step out	❏ Step back
❏ Step forward	❏ Change	❏ Other: _____	

Introduction to the Passage (5 minutes)

Peter was perhaps the most famous of Jesus' disciples. Early on, Peter emerged as the leader of the Twelve. He was a prominent figure in the original Jerusalem church. His story dominates the first half of Acts. He wrote two letters that appear in the New Testament. He is the voice behind the gospel account written by Mark.

Many people identify with Peter. We like Peter. We like him not so much because of his accomplishments but because he is so like us. Not a suave and politic individual, Peter always seems to be putting his foot into it. Not a high-powered executive-type, Peter was a blue-collar fisherman. Not an educated man, Peter relies on others to put his words into print. Not a contemplative person, he was a man of action who did not always plan ahead. In other words, Peter seems to make the same errors we make. He seems to have the same confusion we have. He seems to take the same missteps we take. But in all this "ordinariness" his great redeeming feature is his capacity for love and loyalty. He was loved by Jesus and he responded by giving Jesus his whole life.

We learn a lot about discipleship from Peter, not only when he gets it right, but when he does it wrong. In this story we see both sides of Peter. This is vintage Peter: impetuous, a man of action, full of faith, but then overwhelmed by doubt, fearful and courageous. His story challenges us to a kind of wild, improbable faith that allows us to step into the sort of future we would only attempt because Jesus is calling us to do so.

²²Immediately Jesus made the disciples get into the boat and go on ahead of him to the other side, while he dismissed the crowd. ²³After he had dismissed them, he went up on a mountainside by himself to pray. When evening came, he was there alone, ²⁴but the boat was already a considerable distance from land, buffeted by the waves because the wind was against it.

²⁵During the fourth watch of the night Jesus went out to them, walking on the lake. ²⁶When the disciples saw him walking on the lake, they were terrified. "It's a ghost," they said, and cried out in fear.

²⁷But Jesus immediately said to them: "Take courage! It is I. Don't be afraid."

²⁸"Lord, if it's you," Peter replied, "tell me to come to you on the water."

²⁹"Come," he said. Then Peter got down out of the boat, walked on the water and came toward Jesus. ³⁰But when he saw the wind, he was afraid and, beginning to sink, cried out, "Lord, save me!"

³¹Immediately Jesus reached out his hand and caught him. "You of little faith," he said, "why did you doubt?"

³²And when they climbed into the boat, the wind died down. ³³Then those who were in the boat worshiped him, saying, "Truly you are the Son of God."

Matthew 14:22–33

Analysis (10/15 minutes)

Today's questions are a little different from what you have been used to. They ask you to imagine. Use the data from the text in order to see, hear, and feel what this situation must have been like for the disciples, especially Peter. This is an exercise in imaginative meditation.

1. The Disciples (verses 22–27)
   • Imagine what it must have been like for the disciples to be ushered away from the feeding of the 5,000, into their boat, out onto the lake to battle the wind, and then to meet a ghost who turns out to be Jesus. What was it like? Share your impressions of the sights, sounds, smells, thoughts, and emotions of that scene.
   • What were the disciples feeling about Jesus in all this?

2. Peter (verses 28–33)
   • Imagine what it must have been like for Peter, when he discovers that the ghost is Jesus whom he then asks to invite him to walk on water. What made him do that? What was Peter thinking and feeling when he made his wild request, when he heard Jesus call him to come, when he actually took that first step onto the water, when his single-minded focus on Jesus began to waver and he noticed the wind and waves, when he began to sink, when he cried out to Jesus, when he got back into the boat. Share your impressions of the sights, sounds, smells, thoughts, and emotions of that scene.
   • What did the disciples learn about Jesus through Peter's experience?

Resonance (20/30 minutes)

1. What unbelievable feat have you attempted in the past simply because Jesus called you to do it?

2. What is the name of the fear that has the power to cause you to sink?

3. What act of faith is Jesus now calling you to undertake?

Prayer (5/10 minutes)

1. Go around the group and ask each person to identify in thirty seconds or less one thing God has been saying to him or her personally through this study.

2. Go around the circle a second time and let each person pray for the small group member on his or her right, based on what that person just shared about the impact of the text.

Bible Study Notes

Overview:

Context: Jesus has just fed the five thousand. The crowds are enthusiastic, to say the least. John tells us that they wanted to take Jesus and "make him king by force" (John 6:15). The situation is volatile. This could erupt into an ill-formed, ill-conceived peasant revolt that is sure to end in bloodshed. Jesus defuses the situation by sending his disciples off on to the lake in their boat and withdrawing somehow into the hills. He then reconnects with the disciples in this somewhat unorthodox fashion.

Connection: The themes of this passage are storm, stress, fear, faith, doubt, and worship. In other words, it is a rich passage filled with issues that we too must face as we live the life of faith.

Verses 22–24:

Context: Jesus gives the disciples no option. He "compels" them (this is the force of the verb translated "made") to leave in the boat. Jesus' response to the situation is to withdraw on his own and pray. The disciples, on the other hand, are having a rough time of it, battling against a strong head wind.

Connection: Are we influenced more by the heat of the moment ("Let's make Jesus king") than by listening to what God wants in a situation ("My time has not yet come"). To know God's will takes time, prayer, faith, and the wisdom of others.

Verses 25–26:

Context: Somewhere between three and six A.M. Jesus goes out on to the lake. How he does this is, of course, not clear. That he has power over the elements had already been demonstrated when he instantly calmed the wind and the waves on this very lake (Mark 4:35–41). Even though the disciples know of his power they are still frightened. Of course, at first they do not know it was Jesus. They assume the worst. Who else but a ghost could walk on water? What they feel is a kind of dark terror—the sort of response we have, involuntarily, when we encounter a supernatural being.

Connection: Our fears often drive us. Mostly we fear the unknown, "what might be." When we are afraid, it is a time that we need Jesus.

Verse 27:

Context: In identifying himself, Jesus used an interesting phrase, which can be translated "It is I" but it can also mean "I AM," echoing the great Old Testament name for God (Exodus 3:14; Isaiah 43:10). The disciples are afraid of a ghost when, in fact, Jesus is far greater (and more terrifying) than any mere ghost!

Connection: It is Jesus who is Lord of lords, King of kings, the One who is the Ruler of all powers, the One who is our friend (Ephesians 1:19–23).

Verses 28–30:

Context: Peter tests whether it is actually Jesus by asking Jesus to invite him on to the lake. To Peter's credit, when Jesus calls he comes, despite how outrageous the situation is. To walk on water, who could imagine! He takes that first step on to the water. But then it is as if he says to himself, "What am I doing? I can't walk on water." And he begins to sink. That Peter has faith enough to attempt to copy Jesus' amazing feat says a lot. That he does not succeed because he allows himself to get distracted makes him quite human. Notice that Peter does not attempt this seemingly impossible feat until he hears Jesus invite him to do so. Peter wavers when he "saw the wind." This probably means when he sees the effect of the wind on the water, whipping up waves.

Connection: This is a wonderful picture of a life of faith. Jesus says "Come." We respond. We find ourselves doing what we have never done before, what we could never have done on our own. And it is all right as long as we keep our eyes on Jesus. But when we look down and see the water and feel the wind, we waver. We start sinking and we cry out to Jesus in fear ("Lord, save me") not in faith ("Lord, bid me come").

Verse 31:

Context: In contrast to Peter's great faith (what must it have been like to take that first step onto the water?) is Peter's little faith that results in his sinking (how terrifying to feel yourself go down into the dark, wild water). The contrast in this passage is not between belief and disbelief, but between real belief and inadequate belief. Jesus uses the word "doubt" to describe Peter's state of mind. This is a word that means "in two minds" or "divided in two." The contrast is between having a single-minded focus on Jesus (and thus able to act courageously and do the impossible) and having a divided focus between Jesus and the wind that threatens to overwhelm.

Connection: To be single-minded or to be double-minded, this is the challenge. It is often our experience to be double-minded. Yes, we believe in Jesus but yes, we also believe that the dark powers which feed our fears are able to overwhelm us. Doubt is not always easy to banish. Sometimes all we can do is cry out "Lord, I do believe, help me overcome my unbelief"(Mark 9:24).

Verses 32–33:

Context: When they return to the boat, the wind dies down. The emergency is over. The disciples' response to all this is worship and praise.

Connection: Peter has moved from stress (the hard work of sailing the boat into the wind) to fear (of a ghost) to courage (when Jesus reveals himself and Peter asks to come to him) to faith (he walks on water) to doubt (he sinks) to fear again ("save me") to worship—and all this in a matter of moments! In simple terms, this is the Christian walk: the stress of life, the fear of many things, the courage that comes in the discovery of Jesus, faith in Jesus that leads us to step out in new ways, doubts that assail us as we move forward, the fear that returns, the need to reach out again to Jesus, and worship when we discover anew his sustaining power—all this in a matter of a lifetime!

Small Group Session Ten

Open (20/30 minutes)

Checking In

Begin by checking in with each other. Take up to two minutes to share what you have been learning and hearing as you have worked on the daily lectio experience. Sharing can focus on:

- Where are you in your mastery and use of the lectio process?
- The impact contemplative Bible reading is having on your spiritual life.
- What are you hearing from God?

Group Lectio (30/40 minutes)

Follow the process that is outlined in chapter 1 (page 14). Give some consideration to the role of silence in group lectio. Silence is the soil in which meditation and contemplation grow and flourish. Yet we seldom exercise the gift of silence. Our environment is filled with input of all sorts. Learn to cherish the silence in this process.

The Passage

The passage you will use for this exercise is the dialogue between Peter and Jesus, Matthew 14:27–29.

> Jesus . . . said to them: "Take courage! It is I. Don't be afraid."
> "Lord, if it's you," Peter replied, "tell me to come to you on the water."
> "Come," he said. Then Peter got down out of the boat, walked on the water and came toward Jesus.

Discussion (10/20 minutes)

Continue to share what you are learning. Let the group discussion help your understanding of what God is inviting you to do.

Essay

Step Three: Prayer

Although Step Three is defined as "prayer," you have already been praying in the lectio experience. You began the entire process by praying. You prayed that the Holy Spirit would guide you and be present with you. You prayed as you read over the passage, listening to God's word to you. You prayed as you meditated, asking God for insight into how the text connects with your life. At first glance, it would seem strange to label Step Three as prayer when so much prayer has already taken place. But up to this point, your prayer has largely been an exercise of the intellect and imagination. In this step we move into "prayer of the heart."

This is not prayer for which many guidelines can be given. It is prayer that we learn as we listen to God, as we open ourselves to God.

There is an issue which we must face as we encounter Christ in prayer, namely that such prayer is not always a comfortable experience. While there is a great consolation in prayer, great affirmation, and great love, there is also an underlying tension. Jesus simply will not let us remain in our false selves or pursue destructive tracks even though they may appear attractive to us. We are not just consoled in prayer, we are also confronted.

In prayer we are not simply engaging in some kind of inner psychological dialogue—talking to ourselves, as it were. Theodor Bovet, a highly regarded Swiss physician and psychiatrist, writes of this effect:

> When we think about Christ and call on him, it is not as though we were appealing to a dead or an absent person and deliberating about him: Christ answers, he has an effect on us, he is with us, he is alive. This is demonstrated in the fact that his will confronts us with increasing clarity as an absolute, complete, indeed foreign, will, radically different from our own wills. In those moments when we begin to consider Christ, we usually would like to find in him the confirmation of our own personal will, that is to say his plan should bring ours to the highest degree of perfection. But his will emerges in an entirely different context, with a completely new viewpoint, in contrast to which our will appears to be permeated with trivialities and self-seeking motives . . . .
>
> The abrupt antithesis of Christ's will to ours surprises us; we are vexed by this Otherness ... It can honestly be said that the characteristic of a genuine encounter with Christ is that our initial reaction is to be offended, and have nothing more to do with him . . . .
>
> Here God lays hold of our innermost self. Christ desires that I should tell the definite facts of illness to a patient [in giving this personal illustration Bovet focuses

on his role as a doctor]; I resist this because I do not wish to be altogether truthful with this person. Christ would enjoin me not to attend a certain movie, for I would like to attend it chiefly for the purpose of arousing licentious feelings. . . . Christ thrusts me continually in to the presence of a certain person; I wish always to evade him because I do not like him and cannot forgive him. Right at this point I need to be changed.[1]

William Shannon, in his book *Seeking the Face of God,* compares this type of prayer to "falling into the hands of God."[2] When we read Scripture and meditate on it, we fall into the orbit of God. What happens is that we experience purification—those elements of our false self are revealed and we are moved to let go of them. We also fall into the plans of God, finding our part in it. Finally, we fall into the love of God, knowing God as who he is. This is a potent type of prayer.

What I have described is the goal of step three: deep prayer of the heart. But it is not always the experience we have of prayer when we do lectio. At times we are resistant to what we hear about our false self. We harden our hearts. We stop the process. At other times we are distracted. We move away from the intensity of this sort of prayer. We may not be ready for it. It may be that we simply need more time in order to pray in this fashion. In the end, it is God who gives us prayer. It may be that we need to focus on hearing God's word and meditating on it. Our prayer, then, is really an extension of or a summing up of what we have heard and meditated upon. Our prayer is that we will act upon what we have heard. This is more than adequate. We need to rest comfortably in whatever kind of prayer God gives us.

Daily Lectio

In the week ahead, read through Luke 14:12–24. This is the parable of the Great Banquet with its call to involvement in the world of people.

Introduction to the Passage

In Luke 14:1–24 there is a collection of stories about banquets which Jesus uses to teach various lessons. In the first story (verses 12–14), Jesus teaches about generosity. Jesus encourages the invitation of the misfits of society to your banquet. They will be unable to return the favor (i.e., invite you to their banquet—they won't be having one!). In this way, your reward is in heaven, not in receiving an invitation in return to a banquet staged by one of your guests.

This bit of advice sparks a comment from one of the guests who points out that there will be a great banquet in the kingdom of God. In response, Jesus tells a parable in which the question is raised: would you actually attend such a banquet or would you allow other concerns to sidetrack you? In this parable (verses 15–24), the host has issued invitations which have, apparently, been accepted. But then when he finishes preparations and sends his servants around to tell the guests that everything is ready, they make excuses for not coming.

Jesus identifies three novel excuses. In the first instance, a man pleads that he must go off to see the field he has just bought—as if anyone would buy a field sight unseen. The second man says he has to try out his new oxen—as if this test of their abilities could not wait. The third pleads that he must remain at home because he just got married. This is a reference to Old Testament law that allows a man to avoid military service for the first year of his marriage. It says nothing about avoiding social contact. In response, the host scours the poorer sections of the city and invites the downtrodden. When not enough are found there, he widens the radius of the search to the countryside, giving his servants instructions to "compel" them to come. They will need convincing that they are actually being invited to a grand banquet.

In this way Jesus defines the mission of the church: to invite people to God's great banquet; both those inside the city and those outside the city. As such, this parable speaks to our own part in issuing such an invitation. It is not by accident that our work is to be among the needy and outcast. To follow Jesus is to engage in his work. It is to move beyond a life of safety and comfort with the message of Jesus. Another point of this parable is that we must not resist this gracious invitation by getting sidetracked with lesser concerns.

Work through this passage using the lectio divina method of study and prayer.

---

[1] *Have Time and Be Free* (London, S.P.C.K., 1965), pages 29–32.

[2] *Seeking the Face of God* (New York: Crossroads, 1990), page 94.

The Empowerment of Love

Overview

In the first small group session you get to recall encounters with love—both real and imaginary! This will be good background for your study of Paul's prayer about love in Ephesians 4:14–21. Here you are reminded that the spiritual life is empowered by the triune God. It is God the Holy Spirit who works in our hearts, God the Son who dwells in our innermost being, and God the Father who fills us with his fullness. The group lectio passage is Ephesians 3:17–19. Paul's prayer is that we might grasp the breadth of God's love. The focus of the essay is on the fourth step in contemplative Bible reading: contemplation.

Small Group Session Eleven

Open (20/30 minutes)

Encountering Love

We all know love in one way or another. It is our experience of being loved that sets the tone for how we think, feel, and act in life. We do well to remember our positive experiences of love as we live in God's love.

1. Which of the following events conjures up images of love for you? Describe the scene to the group. By the way, in describing the scenario, you have to include the partner or people involved!
   - ❑ a candle-light dinner
   - ❑ a family picnic
   - ❑ a beach in the tropics
   - ❑ a quiet evening with books and music
   - ❑ a back rub
   - ❑ praise for a job well done
   - ❑ a sleigh ride together
   - ❑ a silent retreat
   - ❑ an unexpected gift
   - ❑ a rousing game of charades

2. In what ways did you experience love as a child?
   - ❑ by being given time
   - ❑ by being made to feel important
   - ❑ by being taken seriously
   - ❑ by being given attention
   - ❑ by being taken places
   - ❑ by being affirmed
   - ❑ by being given things
   - ❑ by being listened to
   - ❑ by being taken care of
   - ❑ by having fun with friends and family
   - ❑ by knowing I delighted people

3. In what ways have you experienced the love of God?

Introduction to the Passage (5 minutes)

Ephesians is a remarkable piece of writing. Samuel Taylor Coleridge, the English poet, calls this epistle "the divinest composition of man." In this letter Paul struggles to articulate the great thing God has done in Christ Jesus to remake the world through the power of the Holy Spirit. There is a grandeur to this book, dealing with the purposes of God for the world, the subduing of hostile cosmic powers, the reconciling work of Christ (whereby the bitterest of enemies are brought together), and the creation of a new humanity and a new society.

In the midst of all these themes we find our place in Paul's vision—we are members of God's family and in touch with God's love. This drives the spiritual life: knowing that we are in Christ and that Christ is in us. Our aim in the spiritual life is to be in touch with God the Father through Jesus Christ by power of the Holy Spirit. Read Paul's great prayer in which he captures the essence of the spiritual life.

[14]For this reason I kneel before the Father, [15]from whom his whole family in heaven and on earth derives its name. [16]I pray that out of his glorious riches he may strengthen you with power through his Spirit in your inner being, [17]so that Christ may dwell in your hearts through faith. And I pray that you, being rooted and established in love, [18]may have power, together with all the saints, to grasp how wide and long and high and deep is the love of Christ, [19]and to know this love that surpasses knowledge—that you may be filled to the measure of all the fullness of God.

[20]Now to him who is able to do immeasurably more than all we ask or imagine, according to his power that is at work within us, [21]to him be glory in the church and in Christ Jesus throughout all generations, for ever and ever! Amen.

Ephesians 3:14–21

Analysis (10/15 minutes)

It is one thing to analyze a story; it is another to analyze an essay. Today we look at an essay—a prayer, really, but in essay form. We need to spend more time than usual making sure we have understood what Paul is saying because this is a content-filled piece of writing.

1. What are the two main things Paul prays? (You will need to sort out all the clauses to get to his main point in each petition.)

   - "I pray that ..." (verses 16–17a) _____

   - "I pray that ..." (verses 17b–19) _____

2. Paul prays that each member of the Trinity will work in their lives.

What does he ask that each will do:

• The work of the Holy Spirit (verse 16): _____

• The work of Christ (verse 17): _____

• The work of the Father (verse 19): _____

3. What is the role of power in the life of the Christian?

4. What is Paul's view of God that emerges in this passage?

Resonance (15/30 minutes)

1. What do you learn about prayer from Paul's prayer?

2. Describe what you have learned about the love of God and the fullness of God in your walk as a Christian.
   • How does knowing that you are loved in such an overwhelming way affect how you think about life?
   • What does it feel like to encounter this love?
   • In what ways does the awareness that God loves you affect how you live?

3. Spend a few moments writing your own prayer for inner strength and inner knowledge. Base your reflections on this passage.

   I pray that ...

Prayer (5/10 minutes)

1. Go around the group and let each person pray the prayer he or she composed, asking for strength and knowledge.

2. End by all praying together, in unison, this great prayer of Paul's.

Bible Study Notes

Overview:
Context: Paul is obviously a very bright, very well educated man. In fact, some would say that his synthesis of Greek and Hebrew thought (as in Romans, for example) ranks among the major intellectual achievements in history. But Paul is no cold-blooded rationalist who is only interested in ideas about God. He is a passionate lover of God and companion of Jesus Christ. We catch a glimpse of this side of his nature in these verses. This prayer is mostly one long sentence in the original Greek (verses 14–19). It is as if the words just tumble out, and grammar is forgotten. He has already done this same thing in the beginning of the letter. After the greeting (1:1–2), the blessing and prayer which follows consists of two very long Greek sentences (1:3–14 and 1:15–23). When Paul talks about God he writes as if he were in a rapture. He is passionately intellectual.

Verses 14–15:
Context: Jews typically stood to pray but they knelt at times of great distress or deep feeling. Clearly, there is a devotion and a fervency about Paul's prayer. It expresses his deep feeling about how he understands the work of God in the world in creating this marvelous new family. In chapters one and two of Ephesians Paul describes the amazing deed of God in creating a new body (the church) out of old enemies (Jews and Gentiles) and that one becomes part of this body (family) by being changed from within. This is a family which exists in two places: in heaven (the church triumphant) and on earth (the church militant).

Paul addresses this prayer to "the Father" whom he sees as the one "who is over all and through all and in all" (4:6). God's family derives its identity from his name. A name in the first century world was more than simply an arbitrary means of distinguishing between people. A name expressed identity. The fact that the family derives its name from God means that the church bears God's identity, is under God's protection, and partakes of God's power.

Connection: To follow Jesus is to be part of God's family. It is to bear the mark of God. Family membership brings family obligations, namely to live in God's way. This is a high and a rich calling. How would we live if we were constantly conscious of being God's people?

Verses 16–17a:
Context: Paul asks that Christians be fortified (invigorated) in their inner being by the Holy Spirit. He asks that they experience the awesome power of God. Having been empowered in this way, they are able to grasp the awesome love God has for them (verse 19). In other words, inner power makes inner knowledge possible. The inner being to which Paul refers is the deepest part of human personality, the place where a person's true essence is found. Paul makes the claim that Christ actually dwells in us. It is this inner reality of Christ that makes possible communication with and relationship to Christ. The word "dwell" means "to take up permanent residence."

Connection: In the spiritual life we do not strive to make contact with some outer being. It is Christ within us. Paul stresses in many places in his writing the fact that Christ dwells in us. He refers constantly to "Christ in us" and to our being "in Christ." To follow Jesus is not just to follow the teachings of Jesus or the spirit of Jesus. It is to be in relationship with Jesus.

Verses 17b–19a:

Context: Now Paul prays for knowledge, specifically for the Ephesians to have the ability to grasp what the love of Jesus is all about. The Christian is rooted in this love—i.e., anchored firmly in the soil of love—and is established (grounded) on the foundation of love just like a well-constructed house. He prays that Christians will have the power to know all this. Paul struggles even to express in words the nature of this love. He uses analogies to do this. In the end Paul has to admit defeat in his attempts to express this reality in words. This is a love that surpasses knowledge.

Connection: It is one thing to acknowledge that God loves us; it is another to know this amazing fact in our bones and in our hearts. In fact, on one level, this is what the spiritual walk is all about: to experience the love of God in an ever-deepening way. This is something that we know, a little bit at a time, over time. We let down our defenses and open ourselves to this love. Lectio divina is a way of opening up to the love of God.

Verse 19b:

Context: It is hard to grasp what Paul seeks to express here for Christians. Again, it is a problem of language. If the phrase "the fullness of God" is interpreted one way it refers to the gifts of grace which God gives to people. Interpreted another way (and either way is possible grammatically), then God's fullness refers to that which fills God himself. In fact it is probably this latter meaning which is intended. Christians are to be filled with the very perfection of God himself!

Connection: No wonder Paul struggles with language. Who can understand what it means to be filled with God! This is the challenge of the spiritual life—to move deeper and deeper into the experience of the love of God and the fullness of God. This is a lifelong venture.

Verses 20–21:

Context: Paul prays this way because he knows God can do all this and so much more. We cannot even imagine all God can do. The word translated "immeasurably more" is Paul's own word. As best we can tell, he made up this Greek word in his struggle to get language to express the reality of God. This is a "super-superlative" word according to one scholar.

Connection: Paul's confidence in God shines through in this passage as does his understanding of God. Paul articulates a very hopeful picture of God (as opposed to those descriptions of God that picture him as a distant, disinterested tyrant). We are made members of God's family. We are filled with God's love, power, and fullness. What a vision of reality.

Small Group Session Twelve

Follow the normal outline for the second session and do a group lectio exercise. What follows here is the more familiar outline for group lectio.

Open (20/30 minutes)

Checking In

Begin by checking in with each other. Take up to two minutes each to share what you have been learning and hearing as you have worked on the daily lectio experience. Sharing can focus on:

- where you are in your mastery and use of the lectio process
- the impact contemplative Bible reading is having on your spiritual life
- what you are hearing from God

Group Lectio (30/40 minutes)

Follow the process that is outlined in chapter 1 (page 14). Consider how you pray. What kinds of prayers do you offer to God? How does the text stimulate prayer? How does that prayer then connect back to your life during the week?

The Passage

The passage you will use for this exercise is from Paul's prayer in Ephesians 3:17–19.

> I pray that you, being rooted and established in love, may have power, together with all the saints, to grasp how wide and long and high and deep is the love of Christ, and to know this love that surpasses knowledge—that you may be filled to the measure of all the fullness of God.

Discussion (10/20 minutes)

Follow your normal pattern.

Essay

Step Four: Contemplation

The goal of lectio divina is contemplation: the communication of love between God and us. This is a form of communication that is too deep for words. Contemplation is resting prayer; it is entering into the presence of God and simply waiting. It is prayer that we cannot control. It is prayer that is up to God. Contemplation is being, not doing.

We tend to speak of meditation and contemplation as two words for the same thing. In fact, they are quite different. Meditation is a mental exercise. It is a natural process which we use for spiritual purposes. Contemplation is a spiritual experience. It is not a natural process nor can it be conjured up by us. It is a gift from God. Meditation involves the use of natural senses and faculties. Contemplation goes beyond all sense and faculty. While we know what to "do" when it comes to the first three steps in the lectio process, the only thing we can "do" when it comes to contemplation is simply rest in silence. It is God who does the doing.

In fact, contemplation is a form of relationship. It is the experience of being with the Beloved. It is the normal residence of those who seek the love of God.

> We have been taught as Christians, and presumably have believed, that "we are created for union with God"—but in practice we seem not to dare to accept the full implications of this on a subjective level, to really embrace it as the central truth of our lives. Least of all, perhaps, are we prepared to trust that this is God's passionate desire for us. (How frustrating, for the Lover!)
>
> At best, perhaps, we vaguely accept that somehow, somewhere, "in heaven," we will come to this union of love. But Jesus' life and teachings concern our lives here and now: "The kingdom of heaven is within you"... "Repent, and believe the good news": you are beloved of God! His message is that we love him in loving one another, and that love is the love of God, living and loving through us in this world, as its source, meaning and end.
>
> It is this love which becomes experiential in contemplative prayer, and gradually informs our lives to become more and more a presence of God's love in the world.[1]

In the end, contemplation is all about awareness—awareness of what really is. It is a state of being, not a state of doing. Most of the time we are not aware. We can walk beside a rugged mountain range, along a trail, beside a brook, and the whole time we are thinking of the latest mystery novel we are reading. We are in conversation with a friend but our concentration is on the bills we have to pay and our fear that we will not be able to do so. Our decision as

Christians is to become aware in ordinary life and in the spiritual life. Shannon identifies some of the obstacles that hinder us from being aware of God, of the world around us, and of other people:

- **Preconceptions:** We see what we expect to see. If we do not anticipate that we will connect on a deep level with a particular person, chances are we do not connect. If we do not expect to meet God in any way except through our thoughts, chances are we will not be aware of God's presence in the center of our being.

- **Preoccupation:** We live in the past (with our regrets) or in the future (with our anticipations) but we let the present slip by unnoticed. We get distracted by lesser concerns. We live fragmented lives. No wonder we find it difficult to focus on others or on God in the kind of way that allows us to connect.[2]

We cannot manufacture contemplation but we can be silent and aware. We practice step four by remaining silent before God—not thinking, not thinking about not thinking, just resting. Silence is difficult enough for us to achieve in our overstimulated world. It will be enough simply to stay in the silence.

Daily Lectio

In the week ahead, work through 1 John 4:7–21, John's powerful reflection on the nature of love.

Introduction to the Passage

The First Letter of John is a powerful document. In it you get the sense that the Apostle John, now an old man and the last surviving member of the Twelve, is summing up what God has been trying to reveal to humankind for centuries. "Here is what it is all about," John says. "This is the essence of the gospel." In particular John makes two statements about God. First he says: "God is light" (1 John 1:5). To say that God is light is to affirm that God stands for truth and purity. God illuminates. God is holy and righteous. Second, he says: "God is love" (1 John 4:8,16). To say that God is love is to affirm that at the foundation of the universe one finds love, not hatred. The God we follow is a God of compassion and companionship, one who gives himself for others.

Neither of these statements was a common assumption about God in the first century. In fact, quite the opposite was true. God was not connected to truth much less purity. Nor was God loving. The gods were understood to be sneaky and dark, up to all sorts of schemes in which human beings were mere playthings, and given over as much to evil as to good. The gods were to be avoided not courted. Thus John's assertion about God was "good news," in fact, it is the best of news.

In this passage John explores the implications of saying that God is love. For example, he tells that we must love one another. This is God's way. He tells us that when we love, we reflect who God is. No one can see God directly but it is in our acts of love that we display God to others. He tells us that the ultimate demonstration of God's love is the sending of his beloved Son to die for us. He tells us that God's love is made complete in us; that love casts out fear, that we love because we have been loved, that we cannot love God if we hate others. This is a passage worthy of much study and application. It is a passage that will change our lives as we learn its lessons and live them out.

Work through this passage using the lectio divina method of study and prayer.

---

[1] *Too Deep for Words: Rediscovering Lectio Divina* by Thelma Hall (New York: Paulist Press, 1988) page 2.

[2] *Too Deep for Words*, page 115. See also the chapter entitled "Noticing God" in the second volume in this series: *Spiritual Storytelling: Discovering and Sharing Your Spiritual Biography*. In this chapter I explore various ways of knowing God.

The Lifestyle of Spirituality

Overview

In the first small group session you get to share the meaning of your names with each other. This will help you think about the power of names and the way in which your name is your identity. The passage you will study is 1 Peter 2:9–12; 3:8–9 in which Peter tells the persecuted believers their true names before God and then invites them to live in a way that reflects this identity. In the second small group session you will skip the usual open exercise in order to have time for a farewell to conclude the small group series. The group lectio passage is 1 Peter 2:9–10, our identity in God. The focus of the essay is on the outcomes we can expect from contemplative Bible reading.

Small Group Session Thirteen

Open (20/30 minutes)

Names

Names are supposed to be neutral things, tags that enable us to distinguish one person from another. But we know that they are more than that. Our names can define who we are, describe how we are connected to our family, or even determine what we do in life.

1. What does your first name mean, if you know, and how do you feel about your name? (For example, Joseph means "may God add sons," Kate means "pure heart," and Jonathan means "gift of God.")

2. What does your family name mean, if anything, and how do you relate to it? What does it say about your origin, family background, social group, era in which you were born, etc.?

3. Have you ever had a stage name, a pen-name, a nickname, another name, a professional name, or an alias? Share the story behind the name.

Introduction to the Passage (5 minutes)

In this passage Peter defines for us who we are in Christ and how we ought to live as his followers. Peter first lists a series of titles drawn from the Old Testament (primarily from Isaiah 43:20–21 and Exodus 19:5–6) which once were applied to Israel but now also belong to the church. Each title builds on the previous title so that the end result is an awe-inspiring statement of identity. Then Peter moves directly into the implications of these titles. For such a people there is a lifestyle implied in their names. Peter is quite specific about this lifestyle. He tells us how we ought to live.

Remember who wrote these words. This is Peter, the same man who asked to walk on water and then sank because of his doubt. That incident occurred at the beginning of Peter's walk as a disciple of Jesus. In this epistle we meet the mature Peter, a man who has lived through much and become a different person than he was before he met Jesus. This passage gives us a hint of what the outcome of a spiritual walk ought to be.

This passage is a fitting conclusion to our exploration of the spiritual life. Peter urges us to live out who we are in Christ in all of life. The spiritual life has sometimes been characterized as an individualistic pursuit that takes people out of the world into their own private piety, unconnected to the needs around them. This is not the biblical view of spirituality. As Peter so clearly states: to know God is to live in a way that declares God. Our spiritual experience must be expressed in our relational life, both with those inside and outside the church. And as we already learned in the parable of the great banquet, we are urged to go into the streets and alleys, to the roads and country lanes to seek out the needy, the poor, the crippled, and the blind. To pursue God drives us to express God in the nitty-gritty of life.

But you are a chosen people, a royal priesthood, a holy nation, a people belonging to God, that you may declare the praises of him who called you out of darkness into his wonderful light. Once you were not a people, but now you are the people of God; once you had not received mercy, but now you have received mercy.

Dear friends, I urge you, as aliens and strangers in the world, to abstain from sinful desires, which war against your soul. Live such good lives among the pagans that, though they accuse you of doing wrong, they may see your good deeds and glorify God on the day he visits us.

Finally, all of you, live in harmony with one another; be sympathetic, love as brothers, be compassionate and humble. Do not repay evil with evil or insult with insult, but with blessing, because to this you were called so that you may inherit a blessing.

1 Peter 2:9–12; 3:8–9

Analysis (10/15 minutes)

1. Find as many "names" as you can in this passage that describe the followers of Jesus.

2. How are the people of God *not* to live?

3. How are the people of God *supposed* to live?

4. What is the connection between who the people of God are and how they live?

Resonance (20/30 minutes)

1. With which of the "names" do you most identify? How and why?

2. What is the challenge for you when it comes to:
   - abstaining from sinful desires
   - living a good life
   - living a harmonious, sympathetic, compassionate, and humble life
   - blessing others and not retaliating

3. How do you understand the nature of the spiritual life as a result of your study of the various passages in this book?

Prayer (5/10 minutes)

1. Go around the group and ask each person to declare one important thing he or she has learned in this small group series.

2. Then end with group prayer in which you thank God for what has been learned, and commit this learning to God. Ask that each person grows as a result, and then commend each other to God in prayer.

Bible Study Notes

Overview:

Context: Peter wrote this letter to bring hope and strength to men and women who were being persecuted because they were Christians. This was the first wave of persecution directed at the church. For the first three decades of its existence the church had been protected, not persecuted, by the Roman Empire. It was seen as a Jewish sect and all the rights guaranteed to recognized religions were extended to Christianity. But that changed in A.D. 64 when Rome burned. The emperor Nero blamed the Christians (contemporary historians recorded that it was Nero himself who burned down Rome so that he could exercise his passion for building). After the fire Christianity was declared a forbidden religion and the persecution started. What Peter says to these persecuted Christians is that they should rejoice in the midst of their suffering because of who they are and the hope they have. He goes on to give very practical advice about how to live in a setting of persecution.

Connection: We are not usually persecuted for our Christian faith (though this is not the case in some places in the world). In fact, to be a Christian is no longer a negative. But what do our lives say about our faith? What message do we communicate through our actions and attitudes? Peter challenges us to let our spiritual side show through by our lifestyle.

Verse 9:

Context: Peter lists four titles which describe Christians. First, they are "a chosen people." They have been chosen to be part of God's kingdom and members of his family. Second, they are a "royal priesthood." The function of priests is to mediate between God and the people. But no such elitism exists in the Church. All Christians are members of this royal priesthood. Third, they were declared to be "a holy nation." They are not "holy" in the sense that they are paragons of virtue. They are "holy" in the sense that they have been "set apart" (which is the root meaning of the word) by God for his service and sustained in that service by the Holy Spirit. Fourth, they are "a people belonging to God." They are precious to God and an object of his care.

Connection: To be chosen gives us a secure sense of belonging in God's kingdom. God wants us as part of his family. To be a priest assures us that we can approach God. We do not have to go through others. To be members of a holy nation declares that we have a job to do for God.

We sometimes think of the spiritual life as a solitary walk with outcomes that benefit those who choose this path. But the fact is, we are part of a great company and as members of this holy nation we have a task to fulfill. We are to declare who God is to the world. We are to invite others to join this happy company, this worldwide community. We are to serve others in God's name.

Verse 10:

Context: In verse 9 Peter contrasts what they once were as a people with what they have now become. The language he uses here is drawn from the prophet Hosea. It refers to the fact that the Gentiles (all non-Jewish peoples) have now become the people of God and recipients of mercy.

Connection: We need to remember who we were before we met God, to know the riches of his present grace.

Verse 11:

Context: Peter draws another contrast that helps them grasp their true identity. They may be a holy nation and royal priesthood in God's kingdom, but from the perspective of the world around them they are nobodies.

Connection: Here is the challenge: to live out what we are. It is well and good to be pious in private, and enjoy a spiritual relationship with Christ. But if this inner experience does not translate into an outer lifestyle it cannot declare the praises of God.

Verse 12:

Context: They are to abstain from those actions and attitudes that work against their souls. To give themselves over to these sinful desires is to harm their inner person. Peter urges them not only to abstain from sin (the negative) but to give themselves to that which is good (the positive). This advice has a practical tone to it. The pagans around them will find it much harder to persecute good people than those who are leading evil lives.

Connection: We cannot live a divided life: in love with God during our devotions and controlled by the world the rest of the day. Our sinful desires corrupt our souls. This spills over into our inner being and will have an impact on our spiritual pilgrimage. The goal is a wholistic life with continuity between our inner and outer lives.

Verse 8 (chapter 3):

Context: Having identified in the previous verses what they are not to be, now Peter identifies what they are to do. He identifies five attitudes and actions to define how they should treat each other in the church.

Connection: We have not done a very good job when it comes to the attitudes Peter names. This verse is a strong challenge to members of the community of faith. The validity of our spiritual pursuit must begin to show itself in our lives in community.

Verse 9 (chapter 3):

Context: Peter turns from the question of how they are to treat others in the Christian community to how they should act toward those who are persecuting them. His basic advice is that they are not to retaliate. Instead, they are to bless their persecutors.

Connection: Our experience in the pursuit of God must make itself known not only in the church but also in the world. Specifically, we are called to be people who bring blessing to those around us. Our spirituality must be expressed in all areas of life. Again, this is a call to a wholistic lifestyle.

Small Group Session Fourteen

Since this is your final session together, divide up your time in the following fashion:

- *Group lectio* (30/40 minutes): Skip the usual check-in exercise and go straight into your final group lectio experience.
- *Discussion* (10/20 minutes): This is a summary of your experience in the whole lectio process and what you have gained from it.
- *Farewell and prayer* (20/30 minutes): Say goodbye to each other even as you plan your next small group experience.

Group Lectio (30/40 minutes)

Follow the process that is outlined in Chapter One.

The Passage

The passage you will use for this exercise is Peter's statement of our identity in 1 Peter 2:9–10:

> But you are a chosen people, a royal priesthood, a holy nation, a people belonging to God, that you may declare the praises of him who called you out of darkness into his wonderful light. Once you were not a people, but now you are the people of God; once you had not received mercy, but now you have received mercy.

Discussion (10/20 minutes)

Use this time to have one final discussion of the contemplative Bible reading experience:

- Summarize your experience of the lectio divina process. Was it easy or difficult? Useful or not so useful? How do you intend to use this process now that the group is ending?
- What is one key thing you have heard from God during this whole experience?

Farewell (20/30 minutes)

Discuss the next step for your group. Here are a few possibilities to talk through as a group.

- **SPIRITUAL DISCIPLINES series:** Take a short break as a group (two weeks) and then start up again and work on another spiritual discipline. There are four other books in this series. The next one in the sequence is *Meditative Prayer: Entering God's Presence* in which you will consider various ways of prayer. This is a natural follow-on from the lectio style of prayer you have been using. The other three topics in the SPIRITUAL DISCIPLINES series are: spiritual journaling, spiritual autobiography, and spiritual transformation. Call Pilgrimage Publishing at 1-800-476-8717 for details.

- **Bible study:** You might want to continue to meet as a small group but switch to Bible study. Call Pilgrimage Publishing at 1-800-476-8717 for suggestions of materials to use.

- **Retreat:** Go on a retreat together. In most locales there are retreat centers that allow you to do silent retreats or guided retreats. This is a great way to deepen your relationship with God.

- **Multiply:** If this has been a meaningful experience for you, why not start other contemplative Bible reading groups? Work together in teams and recruit new members. Help others learn this way of studying Scripture. If you feel the need for more training as small group leaders, call the Pilgrimage Training Group at 1-800-477-7787 to find out the date and time of a one-day seminar in your area.

- **Teach:** Teach the process of contemplative Bible reading in a Sunday school class or during a one-day seminar.

- **Conclude:** It may be time to bring to a close this particular group. If you do, you might want to discuss the plans for growth on the part of each member. You might also want to plan a reunion dinner scheduled in a few months.

Say good-bye to one another in a way appropriate for your group.

- **Group prayer:** Join hands and spend time in prayer together committing the whole experience and each person to God. Or . . .

- **Affirmation:** Focus on one person. Allow the other group members to express briefly what they have come to care about in that person (e.g., his or her courage, honesty, ability to empathize, commitment to ministry, ability to love, practical good sense, friendliness, wisdom). Then gather around that person, lay hands on him or her and pray God's blessing on that person. Or . . .

- **Liturgy:** Prepare a final liturgy (as a group or by assigning this task to one or two people) using both the ancient prayers of the church and new prayers written for the group. Use this as the final experience together.

Essay

Outcomes of Lectio Divina

What is the result of all this? What is the value of lectio divina? For one thing, we need to distinguish between short-term gain and long-term gain. In the short term what we gain from contemplative Bible reading is a new way of Bible study and prayer—a method that serves us well in our attempt to hear God through Scripture. Also, we will have had a new experience of the presence of God. We will have received guidance from God through Scripture. This can only be an encouragement to us.

In the long term what we hope to gain from contemplative Bible reading is transformation. This discipline has a cumulative effect. Over time we become different people—more open to God, certainly, but also more open to others and their needs and more aware of the world around us.

We should see differences in our relationships. When we experience God's love for us (as we do in the process of contemplative Bible reading) then we are able to love others more freely. Being loved allows us to love. We should find that we can let go of some of our old hatreds and angers. This is the beginning of healing. We become more aware. In learning to be aware of God we learn to be more aware of others. We become more sensitive to others and this affects how we react and respond. Through lectio divina we will not become perfect but we should become better.

Perhaps the biggest outcome is that Scripture comes alive for us in new ways. Whereas we once read the text to understand it with our minds, now we encounter Scripture in a new way and on a new level. Now we open ourselves to be changed by what we have come to understand. Our encounter with Scripture becomes an encounter with God through prayer. We pray what we read. This is another thing that happens. We pray in new ways. Prayer becomes easier and more natural in that it flows directly out of our reflection.

What you have gained is a new way of approaching Scripture and praying it into your life. In the end what benefits you most is not the rigid application of each lectio step but the acceptance of the basic process into your daily life.

- You learn to approach a passage in Scripture prayerfully, asking God to speak to you through it. There is new expectation when you come to the Bible. You know the power of reading the passage aloud, and you have learned to listen carefully for what strikes you from the passage.
- You learn to mull over what you hear in such a way that you identify how it connects with your life. Meditation becomes a reflex.
- You learn to offer what you discover to God in prayer. Bible reading and prayer become one process.
- You learn to stay open to God in the silence of prayer. You learn about deep resting in the presence of God but do not feel guilty if that does not happen. You know prayer is what God gives you.

So far we have considered the impact of lectio divina on us personally. But this discipline has an impact on those around us as well, as Theodor Bovet states so clearly:

Each teacher, each worker, each statesman, who does not listen to God, but rather is bound to a divisive system, denotes great danger for many. On the other hand, every housewife, every laborer, or every doctor who listens to God, disseminates love, joy, and peace round about himself, and God accomplishes through him his triumph in the world.[1]

In the end, however, the old monks are right. We seek God in this way because it is our calling to seek God. We do not necessarily become happier or richer or even more fulfilled because we practice lectio divina. But then, these have never been the measures of success in God's kingdom. We will, however, know God better and experience his love as a reality in our lives and not just as a concept we espouse.

Daily Lectio

In the weeks ahead, work through Luke 15:11–32, the parable of the Prodigal Son with its call to return home to family and father.

Introduction to the Passage

There are three main characters in this story: the prodigal son, the older brother, and the father. Each person's story merits our attention in that each story reveals something about us which we need to know in order to become whole people.

There is in each of us a prodigal part that wants to live high, and do self-indulgent sorts of things that break the rules and squander resources. The way this prodigal part is expressed varies from person to person. For some, the rebellion is direct, evident, and destructive. For others, the prodigal part is more hidden. It comes out in dark and devious ways while maintaining a front of respectability. What part of you wants to leave home and live in a far country?

We are also like the older brother who stayed home. He worked hard, played by the rules, and lived as an obedient son. But he came to resent this. He too wanted a party. Even though his father's estate was all his, he felt he was taken for granted. He became remote, angry, and probably a bit self-righteous. What part of you is obedient and conforming and wants to be recognized and rewarded?

There are also elements of the father in us. The father loved his two children—so much so that he allowed his younger son to have his half of the estate even though he knew it would be misused. The father expressed this love by the party he gave when his lost son returned and by the awareness he had that the older son stood outside the celebration. To both sons he gave love and blessing. What is the welcoming, rejoicing, blessing part of you and how can this be expressed?

You may find that your identification is stronger with one party. If this parable connects with you, you may want to read Henri Nouwen's fine book *The Return of the Prodigal Son* (Image Books, 1994) in which he explores each story with wonderful perception.

Work through this passage using the lectio divina method of study and prayer.

---

[1] *Have Time and Be Free,* by Theodore Bovet (London: S.P.C.K.), page 56.

What It's All About: An Introduction to the SPIRITUAL DISCIPLINES Series

Four themes weave their way through the five books in the SPIRITUAL DISCIPLINES series:

Story

We all have a story. Our stories give us identity. They tell who we are since they chart the unfolding of our lives and all the factors that make each of us unique.

But we do not always know our stories. There are various reasons why our stories are murky or incomprehensible:

- *Inattention:* We let life pass us by. Each day comes and then goes, and we hardly notice. Since our minds are not focused on what is happening in and to us, our days go unrecorded.
- *Pain:* Our lives are too painful to notice. Not noticing is our way of coping. If we noticed we would cry out in agony.
- *No grid:* We do not notice the texture of our lives because we have no categories for talking about our lives. Life just happens.
- *No friends:* We do not know our stories because we have never talked about them with anyone else. Perhaps we are shy, or it may simply be a matter of being part of a group that does not talk about such things. Or we may tell only certain kinds of personal stories (e.g., about kids or a job) but leave most of our lives undiscussed.

Not knowing our stories, we do not understand our stories. In not understanding our stories, our lives are a mystery to us. We do not understand our anger or our needs or even our desires. We cannot anticipate our responses or plan our futures. We are left with only the immediate, the here and now, and that, too, soon passes from our consciousness. Nor do we have any way of making sense of our stories. We do not see our stories as having any significance beyond ourselves. We do not connect our stories with God's story.

Pilgrimage

As Christians we understand that our stories are not random. In fact, to be a follower of Jesus is to walk in his way. This Way is not some vague path. It is a well-marked road first walked by Jesus, the author and pioneer of our faith; then walked by the Twelve and others in the first century; and later walked by countless men and women through time; people from different ages, different races, and different cultures. We have ample records left by our ancestors that tell us of the nature of the Way. To be a Christian is to be a pilgrim. It is to be on a journey. Our story becomes the story of our pilgrimage.

Community

It is by means of our stories that we come into community with others. This is another theme running through these books—the nature and process of community. It is my belief that the basis of community is found in sharing our stories with one another. It is very difficult to dislike or disdain someone whose story you have heard. The uniqueness of Christian community is found in the fact that we actively connect our stories with God's story. We evaluate our stories on the basis of what we read in the Bible. We actively relate to others who are walking in Jesus' way.

Disciplines

The spiritual disciplines are simply ways of living that bring us into conformity with the image of Christ. By practicing these disciplines we train ourselves to respond in Christian ways to life as it unfolds. In particular, the spiritual disciplines keep us alert to the presence of God in our lives.

For those who call themselves Christians, the immediacy of God can get lost in the familiarity of routine. Worship, Bible study, fellowship, and even prayer become ends in themselves, not paths to the presence of God. God's voice is muted. Or it gets covered by unexamined cultural or personal baggage. The spiritual disciplines become a way of sorting out the "voices" that would distract us and keep us from noticing the Voice. They also enable us to communicate with God and to grow in our spiritual lives.

The Series of Books

- *Spiritual Journaling: Recording Your Journey Toward God.*
- *Spiritual Storytelling: Discovering and Sharing Your Spiritual Biography.*
- *Contemplative Bible Reading: Experiencing God Through Scripture.*
- *Meditative Prayer: Entering God's Presence* (available in 1997).
- *Spiritual Transformation: Taking on the Character of Christ* (available in 1998).

The Art of Leadership: Brief Reflections on How to Lead the Small Group

It is not difficult to be a small group leader. All you need is:
- The willingness to do so
- The commitment to read through all the materials prior to the session (including the leader's notes for that session)
- The sensitivity to others that allows you to guide the discussion without dominating it
- The willingness to be used by God as a small group leader

Here are some basic small group principles that will help you do your job.

- *Ask the questions:* Your role is to ask the questions in the study guide. Just read the questions and let various group members respond.

- *Guide the discussion:* Ask follow-up questions (or make comments) that draw others into the discussion and keep the discussion going. For example:
  "John, how would you answer the question?"
  "Anybody else have any insights into this question?"
  "Let's move on to the next question."

- *Start and stop on time:* Your job is to start the group on time and, most importantly, to stop it on time. Certain people will always be late so don't wait until they arrive. End on time. If you don't, people will be hesitant to come again since they never know when they will get home.

- *Stick to the time allotted to each section:* There is always more that can be said in response to any question. So, if you do not stick very carefully to the time limits for each section you will never finish the study. And this usually means the group will miss out on the important application questions at the end of the session. It is your job to make sure that the discussion keeps moving from question to question. You may have to keep saying: "Well, it is time to move on to the next question." You may not be able to ask all the questions. Know the material well enough so that you can select the most important questions and skip the rest. Remember—it is better to cut off discussion when it is going well than to let it go on until it dies out.

- *Model answers to questions:* Whenever you ask a question to which everyone is expected to respond (for example, an open question as opposed to a Bible study question), you, as leader, should be the first person to respond. In this way you model the right length of response. If you take five minutes to respond, everyone else in the group will feel that it is okay for them to take at least five minutes (one question will take fifty minutes for the whole group to answer!). But if you take one minute to answer so will everyone else (and the question takes only ten minutes for the group to answer). Also, by responding first, you model an appropriate level of openness. Remember, the leader should be just a little bit more open than others.

- *Understand the intention of different kinds of questions:* You will ask the group various kinds of questions. It is important for you to understand the purpose of each kind of question:

  ▶ *Experience questions:* These are often the first type of question you will ask. The aim of these questions is for people to recall past experiences and share these memories with the group. There is no right or wrong answer to these questions. Such questions facilitate the group process by:
    - getting people to share their stories with one another.
    - being easy to answer so everyone has something to say and thus the group conversation begins.
    - getting people to think about the session topic on the basis of their own experience.

  ▶ *Forced-choice questions:* Certain questions will be followed by a series of suggested answers (with check boxes next to each possible answer). Generally, no one answer is correct. In fact, often each answer is correct. By offering options, group members are aided in responding. This also helps direct the response. When people answer such questions, you may want to ask them to explain why they chose the answer they did.

  ▶ *Analysis questions:* These are questions that force the group to notice what the biblical text says and to examine it for meaning.

  ▶ *Application questions:* These questions help the group make connections between the meaning of the text and the circumstances of each person's life.

  ▶ *Questions with multiple parts:* Sometimes a question is asked and various aspects of it are listed below. Have the group answer each of the sub-questions. Their answers, taken together, will answer the initial question.

- *Introduce each section:* It is your job to introduce each section. This may involve:

  ▶ *Overview:* Briefly explain the focus, purpose, and/or topic of the new section.

  ▶ *Instructions:* Explain how to do the exercise.

- *Comments:* Occasionally it will be helpful to the group if you bring into the discussion some useful information that you have gathered from your own study. Never make long comments. Don't allow yourself to become the "expert" to whom everyone turns for "the right answer." Invite comments from others.

Small Group Leader's Guide:
Notes on Some Sessions

Starting a Contemplative Bible Reading Small Group

If you are the group leader, it is important for you to read carefully the section entitled *The Art of Leadership: Brief Reflections on How to Lead the Small Group*. This will help you in small group leadership and you will understand how this small group series has been structured. It will also give you a series of ideas as to how to tailor the material to fit the needs of your group. Then prior to each session, go over the notes for that session (see below).

- *Recruiting members:* All it takes to start a group is the willingness of one person to make some phone calls. When you invite people to join the group, be sure to explain how the group will operate since this is a different sort of small group. See *The Study Guide at a Glance* on page 5, and *What It's All About* on page 85 which explain the nature of this group.

- *Deciding on a schedule:* The best way to use this material is to take two sessions per chapter. In the first session, do the Bible study. This will help the group to understand the passage in depth. Then in the following week, examine a portion of this passage using the small group lectio divina approach. To follow this approach would take fourteen weeks.

If your group does not have that much time there are various options you might choose:

- ▶ Work through a reduced number of chapters. It is suggested that if you choose this option you ought to cover at least chapter 1 (which introduces in detail the contemplative Bible reading process) and chapters 5 through 7. This would take eight weeks. Add other chapters as time allows.
- ▶ Combine both sections of the chapter into a single session. In this case, you would both study the passage and process one part of it using the small group lectio divina method. The drawback to this is that neither the study nor the lectio exercise is given adequate time. Also, a gap of a week between the study and the lectio exercise seems to allow people to approach the passage with a freshness and with their whole being (and not just their mind).
- ▶ Do only the group lectio exercises. The traditional way of doing lectio divina is without the study portion of the exercise so this would work powerfully and teach a new way of approaching Scripture.
- ▶ Do only the Bible study exercises. This would be traditional Bible study but with a stronger emphasis on application.

- *Finding a place:* It is more important to meet in the right sort of place for this small group than for most small groups. The key issue is silence. You cannot do group lectio divina except in a quiet place. This will mean finding a home or a room where children, pets, and the telephone will not interrupt your sessions.

- *Timing:* There are two times given for each session. The first is for groups that are sixty minutes long; the second for ninety-minute groups.

- *Homework:* There are two parts to the work for group members to do on their own:
  - ▶ *Essay:* In each chapter there is an essay on a particular aspect of contemplative Bible reading. These essays expand group members' understanding of each aspect of the process. You may decide to read and discuss these essays together as a group.
  - ▶ *Daily lectio:* Group members will learn this way of Bible reading and prayer by practice. They are encouraged to work on texts during the week between group sessions. The experience of daily lectio can be used as the open exercise each week.

- *Preparing for the first session:* Get enough copies of this book so that each person has one. The book contains all the information needed for each of the small group sessions as well as information on the process of contemplative Bible reading.

- *The special character of session one:* The first session is the most important. During this session those attending will decide whether they want to be a part of the group. So your aim as small group leader is to:
  - ▶ Create excitement about being part of this particular group (so that each person will want to continue in the group)
  - ▶ Give people an overview of the whole series (so they will know where the group is headed)
  - ▶ Build relationships (so that a sense of community starts to develop)
  - ▶ Encourage commitment to being a part of the group (so that everyone will return next week, bringing along a friend!)

- *Potluck:* A good way to launch the first session of any small group is by eating together prior to the session. Sharing a meal draws people together and breaks down barriers between them.
  - ▶ Ask everyone to bring along one dish for the supper. This makes it easy to have a meal for twelve! If you feel ambitious, you might want to invite everyone to dinner at your home. What you serve need not be elaborate. Conversation, not dining, is the intention of the get-together.
  - ▶ The aim of the meal is to get to know one another in an informal setting. Structure the meal in such a way that a lot of conversation takes place.
  - ▶ Following the meal be sure to do the first session in a complete and full form (and not just talk about what you are going to do when the group starts). Your aim is to give everyone the experience of what it means to be a part of this small group.

Introduction to the First Session

- *Welcome:* Greet the group and let them know how glad you are that they have come and how much you look forward to being with them for the coming weeks.
- *Prayer:* Pray briefly, thanking God for assembling this group. Ask God to guide your deliberations and sharing today and during the coming weeks. Pray that God will guide all of you in discovering the power of contemplative Bible reading to grow in your spiritual lives.
- *Group process:* Describe how the small group will function and what it will study. Discuss, specifically:
  - ▶ *Series theme:* The aim is to learn how to do contemplative Bible reading, both in a group and individually.
  - ▶ *Group experience:* Describe how you will alternate between a Bible study one